Rising from the Ashes

An unintended journey
of deceit, betrayal and suicide

Luanna's story:
as told to Nancy J. Robinson

Romans 15:13

Prologue

My name is Luanna.

He called me Lu for short.

We were married 26 years and have two adult children; one away at college, the other recently married.

I've taught second grade for more than 20 years. Everyone knows me as, "The Queen." My classroom is a castle adorned in purple and pink complete with turrets and carousel horses and frogs that can talk and hot air balloons that float across the ceiling in the sky. All of my students will be princesses and princes for one magical year.

By every outside measure my family and I were well off and living the good life in Southern California.

Then, one grey February day, I learned that everything I thought I had, everything I believed about my husband, Richard, everything about our marriage, even about myself, was riddled with lies and half-truths.

The story you are about to read is true. Some of the names and places have been changed to protect the privacy of those who knew of, or played a part in, my story and want to remain anonymous. My hope is that if you see yourself within these pages that you will run, not walk, out of your relationship before it's too late.

July 16, 2010

"9-1-1. What's your emergency?"

"I'm on H... Valley... R...d. Car.. ire..."

High winds and rolling hills interfered with the caller's cell phone signal creating deafening static coupled with spotty reception.

"A car is on fire?" she asked. "Sir, is your car on fire?"

"No." More static. "CAR ... fire."

"Whose car?" The emergency operator covered her left ear pushing the plastic ear piece further into her ear.

"Sir we need to try for a better signal. Are you able to change your location?" The operator heard tires crunching on gravel. OK, at least she knew it wasn't the caller's car on fire. She listened to varying degrees of static until it dulled to the sound of strips of Velcro being pulled apart.

"I'm on ... and Valley Road."

Better. At least she was able to piece together the conversation. The call was coming from an unincorporated area of San Diego County, a remote area that fell under the jurisdiction of the San Diego County Sheriff. In California, 9-1-1 calls made from a cell phone automatically went to the California Highway Patrol and were then routed to the appropriate authorities. Most callers didn't realize they were talking to the CHP when they dialed 9-1-1, especially if using a cell phone from home. The operator punched a button to the left of her console connecting to a sheriff dispatcher.

"I have a male caller, mile marker five, Highland Valley Road, reporting a car on fire. Poor frequency, unclear whose car or if there are injuries."

She returned to the caller. "Sir, the car that's on fire, is it in the road?" she asked, just as she got a *ping* from the cell tower.

"In ... ing lot .... head," he said.

The 9-1-1 operator typed in the coordinates and a county map appeared on a monitor above her call screen. She zoomed in on the blinking red dot. Not much out that way. Just dense brush, coyotes and migrant worker camps hidden far from the probing eyes of border patrol agents. It looked like the road, just east of the I-15, was a link between the freeway and Ramona, a town known for rodeos, wine grape production and budding Future Farmers of America. Except for a smattering of nurseries and growers, there were no homes in the immediate vicinity which, under normal circumstances, would reduce the cause for alarm, but it was July, and the county had been dry for five months with little to no rainfall. Three years earlier the worst wildfire in the county's history burned 369,000 acres, destroyed 1,600 homes, claimed 10 lives and injured 89 firefighters. Both residents and emergency personnel remained on edge, knowing a single cigarette butt tossed from a car window or a spark from a down power line could turn dry brush into a raging inferno.

Using Google Earth the 9-1-1 operator zoomed in on the area. It appeared that a large vacant lot was at the trail head to Felicita Canyon. *Thank God.*

"Emergency vehicles are on the way," she told the caller just as she heard the faint wail of first responders in the background. She heard a series of small pops muffled by the wind, followed by a loud explosion and the swoosh of combustibles. There was a moment of deafening silence and then the caller's horrific screams.

"OH MY GOD OH MY GOD OH MY GOD," his voice a hysterical pitch.

"SOMEONE'S IN THE CAR!!!!"

In the beginning...

My story begins in Glendora, CA, a city in Los Angeles County, where I was a third generation Californian. I lived in the same house for 18 years with my mom, dad and sister. My father had been married before so I had a half brother-and sister who were considerably older and we rarely saw them.

My father was a self-made man who never finished the 9th grade, yet ended up being the CEO of Challenge Butter. Life was good growing up in Glendora in the 1950s and '60s, and I had no reason to believe that what I considered my *blessed life,* would change. Since I was a portfolio, or "trust fund baby" thanks to a great aunt, I wouldn't have to worry about paying for my college education like most of my friends who would attain their degree under a mountain of debt. Mom's Aunt, Anna Campbell, was part of the "Oil Campbell's" from Long Beach, CA. Great Aunt Anna made sure we all had an education fund. When I graduated high school, I was ready to spread my wings and headed south to San Diego. My dad, who was able to retire comfortably at the age of 57, would manage my portfolio.

It was the summer of 1976 when I enrolled at Palomar College and relocated to Escondido, CA, a small city situated in north San Diego County. I had an apartment nearby and it was there I met another tenant, Jerry Hall. Much to the discouragement and disapproval of my friends and family, Jerry and I married three months later. Jerry was in the United States Marine Corps and, at first, our lives seemed idyllic. But Jerry's time with the Corps was coming to an end and I began seeing frightening changes in his personality. He seemed lost and angry, not knowing what to do with his life. Within six months we were going through a divorce. I don't believe either of us were to blame for the failed marriage, I think it was doomed from the beginning. I was born into a family where money was never a problem. Jerry came from a completely different world. He grew up in a small town in Wisconsin where his dad was a brick layer. Jerry wanted to return to Wisconsin and become a mason as well, a move I couldn't see myself making or a lifestyle I could see myself living. Our backgrounds and our goals were just too different. We were too young and too naive.

As the divorce proceedings began I saw a dark side of Jerry. We'd been married only six months but he wanted a piece of my portfolio. When I refused, he became violent. One night I was in the kitchen with my back to the kitchen window. He broke the window in an effort to choke me. Later he tried breaking into my apartment. "Stalking" laws didn't exist back then but I was able to get a restraining order, found a roommate, and was finally able to begin putting my life back together.

I finished my courses at Palomar College and graduated with two certificates, one in special education and one in child development. I wanted to go on to get my teaching degree but didn't have the stamina at the time to continue my studies. I applied for an open position as an aide to a special education teacher at Marcos High School. My divorce became final while I was working with 9th grade Special Education teens.

After my divorce from Jerry things began to settle into a more "normal" routine. Little did I know I was soon to meet Richard Dowell, and once again, my life would change forever. Richard worked as the Career Counselor for Marcos High School at the same time I worked as a Special Education aide. One afternoon my supervisor asked me to go and borrow a typewriter from the Career Counseling office. Note in hand I headed for the administration office, reading it as I walked. The note, written by my male superior, would today spark an array of disciplinary action, but this was the '70s.

"Check this one out," was scrawled on the note above the request. As a newly divorced 19-year-old, I have to admit I was flattered. I asked for Mr. Dowell and handed over the note after introducing myself. I found him charming and handsome despite the fact that he was significantly older than me. There was a spark between us and, before long, Richard was leaving notes and funny cards on the windshield of my car and making sure we'd bump into each other in the lunch room or on campus. I found his gestures endearing and spontaneity kid-like. He was always coming up with these ideas that seemed to come out of the blue, like, "Hey, let's go to Vegas." I wasn't even old enough to drink! But the divorce and the frightening relationship with Jerry left me feeling so sad and *lonely* that Richard's attention was like a desperate fix for an addict.

Although I dated other guys during this time I was truly enamored with Richard. He paid so much attention to me and seemed both worldly and wise. He seemed knowledgable on just about everything, especially current events. Once, when trying to decide what to do over the weekend I said, "Let's do something really *out there*."

"OK, pick something you'd like to do," he said, ready for anything I came up with. That morning I'd read in the newspaper about a KKK rally at a park in Oceanside and suggested we go for the "experience." Thomas Metzger, a resident of nearby Fallbrook and founder of the White Ariyan Resistance, was the Grand Wizard of the Ku Klux Klan in the 1970s, and was scheduled to speak. It had been all over the news and tensions were running high. I was so naive that I never thought through what could happen at such a racially charged event. The evening quickly turned into a riot but I never felt afraid. Richard made me feel safe and protected. He was older, wiser, and people respected him.

Shortly after we met, Richard told me he was married but separated and was going through a divorce. His wife, I learned, had been a Brazilian exchange student he met while living in South Dakota where he owned a bar. After she returned to Brazil Richard decided to sell the bar and begin traveling. His travels took him to South America where he found Denise, married her, and brought her back to South Dakota. I thought his marriage to Denise had been his first. I learned years later that he'd been married for seven years *before* Denise. I think he knew I would find *two* previous marriages questionable, if not unacceptable, and might stop seeing him.

13

Not long after Richard and Denise returned to South Dakota Richard decided he wanted to move to Los Angeles and join the Los Angeles Police Department. He successfully completed his training at the academy but was rejected after taking the department's psychological evaluation. Richard was furious and spent months fighting what he felt was an injustice. He claimed the candidates were put into a room for what they called the "cherry tree" test. Two psychiatrists reviewed the candidates cherry trees deciding if they went into the "yes" or "no" pile. After a year and a half he gave up fighting the rejection and decided to move further south to Oceanside, CA, where his older sister lived with her husband and two sons. Eventually Richard and Denise moved to Escondido where he landed a teaching job.

In hindsight I now wonder if Richard and Denise were truly separated. I never went to his place and there was one Christmas, while we were dating, that I called him and a woman answered the phone. I asked Richard who it was and he said his "ex wife." He explained that she had been very depressed and he told her come over because he was worried about her. The unquestioning, naive, part of me found his sensitivity endearing. Denise died in a violent car accident a month later when she was trying to pass a semi-truck on a dangerous, winding stretch of road near their home. Richard and I were married ten months later, on October 19, 1984.

From the beginning I questioned whether my marriage to Richard was *normal* but didn't have anything to compare it to. I certainly couldn't compare it to my and Jerry's marriage, and there was such a large age difference between my own parents that I rarely saw any intimacy or affection between them. I didn't know how other couples *were* with each other and I was uncomfortable talking to my girlfriends about things as intimate as sex.

There were the other things that nagged at the back of my mind and left me feeling restless. I'd begin changing my clothes or undress to take a shower, and could *feel* Richard there in the bedroom, lurking somewhere in the darkness or from a partially closed closet door, watching me. He never spoke, he just watched. It was creepy. And when we went on vacations Richard would hire a masseuse to come to our hotel room to give me a massage while he sat and watched. *I hated those massages.* Richard kept saying, "Relax... enjoy it," but it felt sleazy laying there naked while some other man rubbed oil all over my body. I begged Richard to stop. *I didn't want them.* "If I want a massage I'll schedule one with the gal at the salon where I have my hair done," I told him time after time. It didn't matter. What Richard wanted Richard got. It seemed an extension of my "wifely duty" an expression he consistently threw in my face.

To Richard, my wifely duty could be explained with one word, "Sex." One night when I was pregnant with Ross I was sick with the flu and running a fever of 102 degrees. As much as I would have loved to climb into bed and sleep, I was taking 23 college units toward my teaching degree, an English 500 class, and struggling to finish a paper that was due the next day.

Richard came into the kitchen where I was working at the table. He wanted me to come to bed. He wanted sex. I couldn't believe it. I told him I was sick and exhausted and waved my hand over the work I had spread out on the table. "I don't care," was his response. "It's your wifely duty."

I came to passionately hate that expression. I tried to be a good wife and mother. I admit I was not a perfect wife, that I did not succumb to Richard's every need or demand. It was one of the things that constantly came up during our 20 years of marriage counseling, that I "couldn't stand" performing my wifely duty. He just couldn't understand that to me the expression was demeaning and degrading.

The early years...

From the start of our marriage Richard had "rules" that didn't make sense to me. His privacy was extremely important to him. He never wanted *anyone* to know his "business," but I never realized the extent of his obsession until our daughter was born. Jill was a very sick baby, born with a congenital heart problem. After an alarming episode that sent me racing to the emergency room one day, I frantically tried to get ahold of Richard at work. When I called his office, not only did no one know he was married, but no one knew he had a daughter. I was first stunned, then hurt, then furious.

That night when I confronted Richard he insisted I was overreacting and assured me that he simply didn't want people at work knowing his business. Again, my *naiveté* came into play. I had, after all, quit my job at the high school when our relationship became public. The 'higher ups' felt an aide having a relationship with someone in administration was inappropriate. I'm fairly certain the 17-year-age difference didn't help.

We never really socialized with any of Richard's co-workers. He told me spouses weren't invited to school district functions. In fact, I think the only function I ever attended was his retirement party when he left the school district after 33 years. I often went alone to my work functions because he just wasn't a social guy.

Richard and I quickly settled into very specific roles as partners and parents. We had two separate bank accounts for our paychecks. My salary paid for groceries, clothing, the children's needs and their activities. Richard paid the mortgage, utilities and car payments from his paycheck. When it was time to start looking for a larger place to live, it was Richard who did the "house hunting" while I stayed home with the kids. I wanted to be part of the decision, but Richard was adamant saying that, *"Bringing you and the kids along would be burdensome."* Richard eventually found a house in Oak Hill, a part of town he loved. "And there's room for a nanny," he said, which I knew sealed the deal because Richard insisted I return to work immediately. He also made it clear that the nanny's salary would come from *my* paycheck.

We were rigid with the kids, although I didn't really think so at the time. They were allowed two activities that they had to stay with for at least six months. I felt this would teach them to not be quitters. They couldn't just start something and change their minds after just a few weeks. I never insisted they become involved in music because I was forced to take piano lessons when I was a child and promised myself I would never do that to my kids. I didn't want other parents yelling at my kids so I shied away from team sports but that changed when a parent of one of my student's coached baseball and talked me into letting Ross join the team. Being a lefty, Ross always got hit so he was known as *"the magnet"* and I was *"the ice queen"* because I was always the runner for the ice packs. Richard attended the baseball games and took stats, something he was asked to do but resented because he said it didn't allow him to watch the game, yet, I can count on one hand the times he played a game of golf with his son. Instead his idea of father/son bonding was to take Ross on a golf trip when he was older. Richard probably went to *two* of Jill's hockey games, so.... Ross also did karate and was actually quite good. By the 8th grade he had two black belts. He also began playing golf in first grade and went into varsity golf his freshman year in high school. He ended up getting a golf scholarship to a college in Kansas but it wasn't a good fit for him and he returned 57 days later to go to school in northern California.

For the most part I was in charge of the kids until they got into high school. Since Richard was a high school teacher earlier in his career it seemed to make sense to let him take over the academic part of their high school years. He drove both of them to school in the morning until they got their licenses and was in charge of the homework. Richard had little interest in their social activities, calling me the social director for the family. I never saw it as a problem until Jill's nanny, Jeri, pointed out that the one day a week, Saturday, that Richard *could* be involved with me and the kids he was always too busy with "errands." I guess I convinced myself that Richard needed his own space. I was, after all, allowed to go visit my "Ya Ya" sisters once a year for three days.

Thanks to my trust fund I was in a comfortable financial state when Richard and I married. Still, he worried incessantly about money, almost to the point of obsessing about our finances. Richard made *all* our financial decisions, even ones I didn't necessarily agree with. When we met in 1978 I was driving a

Datsun 280 Z, a car my dad paid cash for. I was able to drive it right off the lot. It was a gift for my 19th birthday. When I got pregnant with Jill it became harder getting in and out of the sports car. Richard and I talked off and on about whether it would be better to trade in the cars for ones more practical, but the conversations were vague and we never came to a decision. I was stunned the day I came home from work to find my 280 Z gone and replaced with a Mitsubishi Galant. In the place of Richard's Volkswagen was a two-seat black Pontiac Fiero sports car. He quickly covered his actions by saying the Fiero would be our "date night" car.

Why couldn't we have just switched cars until the baby was born? I wondered, but didn't say anything. Still, my reaction mustn't have been the one Richard expected and I immediately chastised myself. He was only looking out for me and the baby. I was brought up in a family where my dad was the boss and made all the decisions. *He* never steered us wrong, so I had to trust that Richard wouldn't either.

Jeri joined us as Jill's nanny when she was about 18 months and stayed with us for a couple years. I decided it was time to quit my job as a buyer at the Mercantile and go back to school so I could finally get my teaching credentials but Richard didn't support my decision. With Richard it was always about the money. But this time I wouldn't back down, so he drew up a "contract" stating I would complete my degree in two years. I signed the contract but that still wasn't enough. He didn't trust the schools, insisting they "dragged out programs to get more money." He made a copy of our contract and insisted it be signed by the admissions counselor at San Diego State University. This would solidify that I would stick to the plan or the deal was off and I would have to go back to work in retail. The counselor found the request odd but I told her it was the only way I'd be allowed to go back to school. Reluctantly, she signed it.

Despite the fact that I used the money from my trust fund to pay for tuition and Jill's childcare, Richard would still wake up in the middle of the night and start pacing. One night I woke up when I felt Richard getting out of bed. "What's wrong?"

"We have money problems, *we have money problems,*" he said as if this was something he'd told me over and over.

As in the past, my response was, "Take money from the trust if we need it." There was at least $200,000 in the account which would certainly cover the expenses of running the household for the time I was in school. The mortgage and car payments were paid from his salary. Everything else was taken care of so I couldn't understand this obsession with not having enough money.

Richard sighed and sat on a chair by the bed muttering more to himself than to me. "I think I need to sell my partnership in the apartments."

I bolted upright.

"What??? What apartments?"

Richard said that right before we got married an acquaintance of his asked if he'd become a partner in the purchase of an apartment complex. *He never told me.* In fact, he kept it *hidden* from me. Where was that account and who was managing *that* money? In fact, who was managing the apartments? Here was additional income I never knew about and yet, despite my salary, my inheritance, my trust, Richard's income and income from rental properties he was still frantic about *"money problems?"*

So how is it that we are always broke? I wondered. And what else don't I know?

I would one day find out.

Chapter One
February 23, 2010

I pushed the door of my classroom open against a heavy gust of wind. Report cards were due the beginning of next week and I was facing several very long nights. I just couldn't seem to focus, couldn't seem to shift from neutral into drive. I had an ominous feeling that something bad was about to happen and my life as I knew it was about to change. For better or worse I didn't know.

It was a gray February day. Intermittent showers forced us to stay inside most of the day and the cold air was such a contrast from the dry air in my classroom that my skin prickled and my eyes watered. Overhead black and blue clouds stretched from the horizon to the sky. Forecasters called for rain by evening.

That puts an end to my evening walk with Kathy, I thought, but maybe that's what was meant to be. I *had* to get started on report cards.

The short distance through Carson Park from the school to the house was littered with leaves and debris. A few branches had broken off the eucalyptus trees and made navigating the road more challenging. When we built the house on Ranch Road years earlier it was for two reasons; the proximity to the elementary school where I taught, and having Carson Park as our back yard. Situated on 185 acres with three ponds and scores of hiking trails, the park was my after work "cocktail."

Although I would have welcomed this abrupt change to San Diego's normally picture-perfect weather, tonight, of all nights, I looked forward to walking with Kathy. I needed someone to talk to and Kathy would be the one. Kathy and I met when her kids were in my second grade class. We developed a friendship that lasted long after the kids finished elementary school. If I could talk to anyone about the unsettling feeling that something was lurking in the dark corners of my marriage, it would be Kathy. I just didn't know how to put into words what was keeping me awake at night. *Everyone loved Richard. The kids loved Richard.* He was a good father, a good teacher, a good worker. He was smart and funny; I heard time and again what a terrific storyteller he was. There were times I wondered if the stories he told were embellished, or even true for that matter, but he could certainly keep people entertained with his storytelling. But I saw a side of Richard that others didn't, and that side frightened me.

A distant rumble of thunder rattled the car windows as I pulled into the driveway and hit the remote attached to the visor to bring up the garage door. *Maybe the weather is Divine Intervention,* I thought. I promised myself to finish at least a few report cards before I resumed my frustrating computer search.

Every evening after dinner I'd been going on the home computer searching for answers to questions I didn't even know. If I *knew* what I was looking for the search would be easier. Still,

I was convinced the answers were somewhere inside that computer.

"Richard?" I heard the squeaking of the office chair overhead and could smell dinner in the oven. My stomach churned. I'd been having trouble eating lately so my meals consisted mainly of hot tea or soup.

"Be right down."

I heard the office chair roll along the hardwood floor above and groan as Richard left the seat. I set the files on the table next to the wet bar and pulled a bottle of Chardonnay from the fridge, pouring the wine into a glass bedazzled with a crown and tiny fake rhinestones. A gift from one of my many room moms.

Richard went to the stove, opened the oven door, and reset the timer. "A few more minutes," he said without turning. I leaned against the door frame studying this man I'd been married to for more than 20 years.

"So what did you do today?" It was the same question I asked every day since Richard retired from the school district six years earlier, and got the same answer.

"Oh, the usual." I didn't move from my spot and instead watched Richard maneuver around the kitchen. After he retired from the Marcos Unified High School District in 2004 as the

"Director of Categorical Programs," we agreed, since he insisted I continue working, that he would make dinner every night and cleanup after so I could prepare for class the next day. Richard spent most of his time alone. Once a month he got together with a few neighbors to play poker but that was about it. He spent most of his days on the Internet or at the library.

"You know… paid some bills, answered a few e-mails, went to the library... " I forgot I'd even asked the question.

"*Really?*" I asked. "Because I was on Orange Avenue this afternoon and drove past the library but didn't see your car. I thought maybe we could grab a cup of coffee.

"I probably already left by the time you drove by," he said transferring the chicken to a platter and taking it to the table without looking at me. For the hundredth time I wondered why he looked so unkempt every time I got home from school, like he hadn't washed his hair for weeks when I knew he showered that very morning.

Dinner consisted of small talk of what was on tap for the weekend, what we needed from the grocery store and what dates needed to be put on the calendar hanging from the side of the refrigerator. I could hardly wait for dinner to end so I could go to the office and continue my search. I'd been praying and praying that the Lord would help me find whatever I was looking for.

"Done?"

"Yes, thanks."

"You didn't eat much."

"I had a big lunch," I said, a lie that went unnoticed. "I need to get to work."

I pushed my chair away from the table, grabbed my student's files and headed for the stairs. One click brought the Macintosh to life. With a heavy sigh, and silent prayer, I began my search.

6:00 p.m.

Please, I prayed hovering the cursor above the menu bar. *Let me find something tonight.* I clicked on the Apple icon, moving the highlight bar down to "Recent Items." As usual the same applications appeared. I clicked on the mail icon and looked over the list of mostly junk mail making a note that I needed to respond to a friend's invitation for lunch and cancel a dentist appointment. Nothing raised a red flag. I leaned back in the chair. The cursor seemed to be taunting me. Although there was only one computer in the house there were three *users* on the Mac. Richard and I used the same password to log in, Ross and Jill still had active accounts so they could use the computer when they were home from school or at the house. What if I was looking in the wrong place? I clicked on "change user" and Ross and Jill's names appeared. Ross had just been home to attend the funeral of a friend who died tragically in a car accident. I knew Ross had been on the computer to check his email and school portal page where assignments were posted from his professors. The cursor blinked in the blank space for "password." I closed my eyes and pressed my fingertips to my eyelids. *Nothing is ever easy,* I thought. I was so weary and felt so helpless… helpless but not hopeless. My faith is strong and I prayed so long and so hard for answers that I believed if there was something I needed to know, God would take me there.

Lord please. I can't handle another dead end. Help me.

I opened my eyes and felt a rush. *The name of Ross's truck.* "Tacoma," I typed. I held my breath waiting to hear the Mac's customary "thunk, thunk" of denial. Instead a tiny kaleidoscope wheel began to spin. When it stopped I was in the belly of Ross's web pages.

I hesitated before clicking on the *Safari* icon that would display Ross's most visited websites. San Francisco State University's website was there, his email page, his bank account, Craig's List (*I wonder what he's looking to buy?*) and then at the bottom, an icon for something called *"The Back Page."* I drew closer to the computer screen, squinting. *Was that a naked girl?* I hovered over the site for just a moment. I felt like a voyeur intruding on Ross's privacy but also I felt that I'd been led here. I also believed that once I opened this door there would be more doors to open, and once I walked through, there would be no turning back. I took a deep breath and clicked once. The page filled the computer screen. What I thought was a naked woman was actually a very young teenage girl in a thong bending over a chair, looking provocatively over her shoulder back at the camera lens. One sentence was typed beneath the photo.

"Married but looking for a good fuck?"

It felt like the air had been sucked from the room. I could actually see the thin fabric of my shirt quivering with my racing heartbeat and felt a thrumming in my ears. I forced slow, deep breaths to keep from hyperventilating, stood and leaned against the railing not trusting my legs to get me down the stairs. I could hear the clanging of the dishes in the kitchen below.

"Richard?" I called over the banister.

He didn't respond so I made my way to the kitchen. "You need to come up and look at something on the computer." My voice was trembling and I willed it to stop. He turned toward me.

"Look at what?"

"You...just....need...to....come." The look on my face must have been enough that he shook the water from his hands, wiped them on a tea towel next to the sink and followed me up the stairs. I pushed past him to take the seat in front of the computer and tapped the space bar. The dark screen sprung to life.

"Look at this."

Richard leaned forward. I could feel his breath on my neck.

"Where are you?" he asked.

"I'm signed in to Ross's account."

"What?"

"I signed in as Ross."

"Why?"

"What does it matter why?"

"How did you *get* there?"

"What?"

He actually sounded annoyed. *Why does it matter how I got here instead of what I found?*

"How did you *get* there?" he asked again, this time sounding angry, as if I didn't understand the question or wasn't willing to provide an answer.

I turned in the chair to look at him. *"Why does that matter?"*

He didn't answer and now it was my turn to be annoyed. I looked at him hard before answering.

"I prayed."

Dozens and dozens of pages filled with photos and personal information of prostitutes for hire filled the screen. Finally Richard spoke.

"Well, Ross must be accessing the home computer from school." He voice was very calm, very matter of fact.

I felt physically sick. "I'm going to talk to him."

"No." his response was immediate and harsh. "*I* will handle this Luanna." With that he turned and left the office. I heard him open and close the refrigerator, returning to the tasks at hand with barely the blink of the eye. Was I overreacting? Why did he seem so nonplussed, so unaffected by what he just saw? I went to the bathroom and ran cold water over my wrists then my face. I couldn't believe Ross would be visiting these sites let alone be communicating with people who were paid for online pornography and sex. I went back to the computer where my discovery was still on the screen. I continued clicking the "next" button until I couldn't stand looking at one more doe-eye prostitute in positions that both sickened and embarrassed me. Some of these girls looked barely out of high school. Some were in their 50's. That's when I saw that the most recent visit was today.

In fact the last visit was just minutes before I walked in the door.

As expected the rain came down as if driven by an angry force. Kathy and I briefly talked and planned to walk the next day. I began to plow through report cards but was afraid to leave the computer, afraid that what I discovered would somehow disappear, so worked from the small keyboard area in front of the screen instead of cross-legged on the bed where I usually worked from my laptop. Finally, as the clock struck midnight I knew I didn't have a choice but to shut it down and try to get some sleep.

Richard was already sleeping when I climbed into bed beside him. Hard as I tried I couldn't keep the questions from looping over and over in my mind. Finally at 3:00 I gave up and went down to the kitchen to make coffee. I was exhausted, and from the sound of the wind and the rain it looked like it would be another day confined inside.

Thank goodness for the assembly I thought as I hurried through the corridor to the computer lab. Jennie, my second grade counterpart, promised to keep an eye on my kids so I could talk to our IT guy. Hopefully Burt would be at his desk and not in some classroom resolving a technical issue.

I stood outside the door for a second and said a silent prayer before knocking. "Come In." *Thank you Lord.*

"Hey Burt," I said closing the door behind me. "Sorry to bother you but I'm hoping you can answer a question for me."

"Sure. Please," he said motioning to the chair beside his desk. "Have a seat."

"Is it possible that something my son is working on at school could show up on our home computer?"

"Not unless he e-mailed something to himself," Burt said. "Let's say, he wanted to be able to work on something at home. He could e-mail it to himself and it could sit there until he opened it on your home computer. Other than that it's not possible. The computers aren't linked to each other."

Like a house of cards I felt my world begin to crumble. There was only one other explanation. Richard. Ross and Jill's *father*. The man I'd been married to for more than two decades. *The father of my children*. The father who just let his son take the fall for his own deviant indiscretions.

My God who would do that? I wondered. And who *is* this person I've been married to for 25 years?

Chapter Two

February 24, 2010

I barely had Patty and her twin brother Joseph out the door and into the arms of their babysitter when I turned off the lights, locked my classroom and hurried to my car. I thought the school day would never end. I had to get home; had to get back on the computer and confirm my discovery, find out how long it had been going on, take notes of website addresses or start keeping some sort of records, something, anything, to confront Richard. My head had been pounding since the computer tech at school told me it was impossible for this to be Ross's doing. Richard so seamlessly, so effortlessly, lied to me.

What else has he been lying to me about?

I shrugged off my jacket and tossed it with my keys and files on the chair beside the door. Since I usually stayed late at school prepping for the next day Richard wasn't expecting me for a few more hours. I needed to do this before he returned from wherever he was. I hurried up the stairs and pushed the button that brought the computer to life before even sitting down. As usual our three names appeared on the screen, mine and Richard's beneath a yellow sunflower, Jill's beneath a Golden Retriever and Ross's under the Chinese symbol for "balance." I typed in Ross's password. The menu bar appeared at the top and then the icons along the bottom of the page. Clicking on the Safari icon I waited for the twelve most recently visited websites to appear. The screen remained blue. I clicked on the Safari icon again. Nothing. *What?* I felt a flutter in my stomach. Something must be wrong. I clicked on File and dropped the cursor down to "Open Recent." The screen remained blank, just a blinking cursor winking at me from a brilliant cloudless sky.

It was as if everything I saw the night before had vanished. No files, no pages, no pornography, no prostitution sites. This couldn't be. Then I felt the first pang of fear. *Oh dear God,* I thought. *He knows. Richard knows that I know; and he made it go away. He erased it all so I could never prove what he's been doing.*

I slumped back in the chair covering my face with my hands. After a few moments I looked again at the empty screen. *Well, he might have been able to physically erase the pages I saw, but he would never,* ever *be able to remove the images from my mind or the knowledge that what I saw was very real.* Why hadn't I expected this? Exposing him would be humiliating, let alone devastating, and could destroy him professionally, as a husband *and father.*

Richard would never let that happen.

He was too controlling; was too much a narcissist. He would never be brought down from the pedestal he'd proudly stood upon for so many years. Suddenly, my scalp prickled, the sensation slowly making its way down my spine. Over the years I'd been the recipient of Richard's anger. Although he never *physically* abused me, the emotional abuse was equally devastating. There were times I'd endure the silent treatment for weeks on end for doing something as trivial as using a red ink pen in the checkbook. I've seen, first hand, the man I thought I knew and loved become a complete stranger when he was crossed.

All of a sudden, *I was terrified.*

I laced my shoes and grabbed a sweatshirt from the back of the door. Kathy wouldn't be meeting me for another half hour but I had to get out of the house. Dinner had been excruciating. Richard came home two hours after I discovered the computer had been scrubbed clean. I'd already exited the program, turning off the computer and monitor, leaving everything as I found it. When Richard returned he found me at the kitchen table, the evening news on in the background, working on report cards.

Acting nervous and jittery Richard started bustling around the kitchen seemingly upset that I was home and dinner wasn't ready. I suggested we just heat up leftovers. I had no appetite and just wanted to be out of the house. As in more recent days and weeks he seemed disheveled and unkempt. He looked *greasy,* for lack of a better word, although I knew he showered that very morning.

I could barely sit at the same table with Richard let alone make small talk. Finally I said, "Did you talk to Ross today?" The silence was longer than necessary and I knew I pissed him off. After what seemed like forever he said, "No, not yet."

"Well, you need to."

"I *told* you Luanna," the harshness of his tone made me flinch. "I will handle this." Without missing a beat I stood, dropped my plate into the sink, and turned.

"Well if you don't... I will." Dinner was over.

I slammed the door behind me and walked toward the park. *What was I going to do?* I was the only one who knew what Richard had been doing. For how long I had no idea, but with no proof, I had no ammunition to confront him. Richard would say I blew everything out of proportion, or worse, that what I saw was all in my head. He was always accusing me of overreacting.

When I saw Kathy's car pull into the lot I stopped and waited for her near the tennis courts. We'd only been walking a few minutes when I turned and realized she was no longer beside me.

"What's the matter?"

"Luanna, I've been talking to you and you haven't heard a single word I've said. What's wrong?" I didn't answer because I didn't know how, or where, to start.

"Come on, Luanna, I know you. I could tell last night on the phone that something was wrong. If you don't want to talk about it I understand but I'd like to help if you do."

The heaviness in my chest was crushing me and I struggled to find the right words.

"I found something on our computer last night."

"What?"

"Pornography. Lots of pornography. Pornography and sites of prostitutes for hire. There wasn't just a few of them Kathy....there were a lot."

"God Luanna." Kathy seemed genuinely shocked.

"I found them on Ross's site, no, it wasn't Ross..." I sounded like a lunatic. I stopped and sat down on the curb. Kathy sat down beside me. "For a long time I've been feeling like something has been terribly wrong with Richard and me, with our marriage. I didn't know what, I could just feel it. So I started looking on the computer for some kind of clue. I could never find anything. Then last night when I hit another dead end something made me think of going onto one of the kids accounts. I switched over to Ross and when I clicked on recent history all these *pages* came up. *Craig's List*, something called *"The Back Page."* Kathy the photos were so horrible. One girl looked like she was still in high school. It said, *"Married but looking for a good fuck?"* Kathy flinched. "I couldn't believe what I was actually seeing so asked Richard to come up and look. He said Ross must have been doing this stuff on the computer at school and it was somehow showing up on our home computer.

"I told Richard I was going to call Ross and he got angry and said he would handle it. This morning I asked our computer guy at school if it was possible for something Ross was working on at school to show up on the home computer and he said not unless he was emailing stuff to himself. This wasn't email. That means it's Richard's."

"Oh God, Luanna, I'm sorry."

I looked at Kathy who seemed genuinely shocked. "Not only did he lie to me but he threw his own son under the bus. *How could he do that?* So today I came home early. Richard's always at the library, or wherever he goes until 5:00. I wanted to copy some of the stuff I found or at least write down the websites so I could confront him, but when I got home it was gone."

"What do you mean it was gone?"

"Gone!" People were turning to look at us sitting on the curb. I took a deep breath. "Kathy, everything was gone, like it never existed. I went on "recent history" and there wasn't any. It was blank. He must have deleted everything. There's no activity showing up at all. It's like it never existed."

We sat there, quiet for a few minutes. I hadn't noticed that it started to rain again.

"Luanna, do you know what *cookies* are?"

"I'm assuming you're not talking about the ones you eat. No, I don't."

"Nothing's ever *completely* removed from a computer. You can delete things so they don't show up anymore but they stay *forever* in the computer's memory. Think of it like a blueprint of every site you've ever visited, everything you've written, every address you've ever entered, every appointment you typed into a calendar. It's all there. All stored on the *cookies* in your hard drive.

"That's why you always see the FBI taking people's computers out of their houses when they're investigating a crime," she said. "They want to see what websites the person has been visiting and what they might have been researching. People *think* they've gotten rid of evidence, but it's still in there.

"Oh God, Luanna," she looked at me alarmed.

"You don't think he's into *child* pornography do you?"

I felt a swooshing in my ears and put my head between my knees to keep from passing out. I'd been so horrified at the images I'd seen that I never considered there could be more. Of course there could be more. The thought made me sick.

"Kathy," I said, looking at her horrified, "If Richard is into kiddie porn and it's on my home computer I could lose my job."

"At the least...." Kathy mumbled.

"What am I going to do?"

"Well, the first thing we're going to do is get those cookies off that computer."

For the first time I felt like I could breathe. There was something unbelievably comforting when she used the word, "We."

Chapter Three

February 25, 2010

Packing up my work for the weekend I looked at the clock and knew I needed to hurry, then stopped and laughed aloud. I was hurrying to not be late for our weekly appointment with our marriage counselor. *What a joke.* From all outside appearances our marriage had no more problems than anyone else's, yet we'd been seeing a marriage counselor for 20 of our 25 years together. I didn't want to be in the same room with Richard let alone sit with him and our therapist pretending to want to work on our marriage. But I decided this would be a perfect way to confront Richard. At least Dr. Heard would be my witness.

Richard and I rarely rode together to our marriage counseling sessions and instead met at the therapists office. But I had to drop my car at the mechanics that morning so Richard was picking me up at school. We didn't speak during the 15 minute drive to Rancho Bernardo. The tension was apparent the moment we walked into our therapist's office. As usual, Richard took his place in the center of the sofa. I sat in a chair across from him next to Dr. Heard.

"What's up?" Dr. Heard asked looking from Richard to me. When Richard didn't say anything I said, "Do you want to tell Dr. Heard what I found on the computer Tuesday?"

"Oh no," Richard said, his voice dripping with sarcasm. "You *love* to tell stories. I'll let you do it."

"Okay," I said, suddenly nervous. "Dr. Heard… for a long time I felt something was wrong with our marriage, above and beyond the issues we talk about here. But I could never figure out what it was. Well, the other night I went on the computer and found these horrible websites."

"Horrible in what way?" Dr. Heard asked.

"There were pornographic sites, lots of them, and prostitutes selling their services. I opened one that said, "Married but looking for a good fuck?…" Richard said it must have been Ross's, but Ross is at school." I paused trying to get my next statement just right. Richard always dodged sensitive issues or avoided telling the truth by saying, "Well, that's not what you asked, Luanna," making it my fault for not choosing the right words. I knew what I said now had to be phrased exactly the "right way" or Richard would slither around the truth.

"I need your help," I said looking, pleading, with Dr. Heard. "I'm trying to ask Richard if what I found on the computer was his doing. Can you help me?"

"Why do you need me to help you? Richard is right here. Ask him."

"Because," I felt my voice falter. "He's always getting around a question by saying I didn't ask it the right way." I realized how ridiculous that sounded but I would not be intimidated by Richard glaring at me in that condescending way. This was too important.

"Just ask him what you want to know," Dr. Heard said again.

I turned to Richard who still sat, legs crossed, one arm casually draped over the back of the sofa, smirking at me like I was a petulant child.

"Richard, were you the one visiting the sites I found on the home computer? The pornography sites and sites of all the prostitutes for hire?"

Richard made a show of taking a deep breath then exhaling slowly as if it were taking every part of his resolve to remain composed.

"I … told … you … Luanna," his voice was stern and measured. "It was NOT me. It was Ross, I imagine. I don't know how you got into that site. I don't *know* how you got his password but this is somehow connected to Ross."

I turned away from Richard and toward to Dr. Heard. "I talked to the computer tech at school and he said, *absolutely not*. He told me it was virtually *impossible* that what Ross was doing on the computer at school could show up on our home computer unless it was something he emailed to himself, but these were not emails. These were frequently visited Internet sites, not email. And now they're gone. When I went to check the computer everything was gone. Everything's been erased..." I felt my throat constrict and was near tears.

"I know what I saw!!" my voice sounded frenzied.

"Well then," Richard said dismissively, brushing away some imaginary lint from his slacks. He was actually *sniggering*. At that moment I knew that to Richard this was a game. And he only played games he knew he'd win. I was furious. "I'm going to ask you one more time..." Richard stood, interrupting me. I actually shrank back.

"Luanna, If you discuss this with me *one more time* ... I'm going to get really, *really*, pissed. Because I have told you, and am telling you for the *last time*, it's nothing *I did*."

I decided to back off. At least it was out there, and Dr. Heard was a witness. Richard was royally pissed and I didn't want to upset him any more than I already had. I still needed to ride home with him, *and I was afraid*. Besides, I already had a plan in place.

After Richard dropped me back at the house I had a Mobile Tech Squad standing by to come and copy the "cookies" off the hard drive of the computer. I had a very small window of time, and I was petrified.

Kathy and I agreed to have the Mobile Tech Squad remove the cookies from the hard drive and send them to Kathy's computer. It seemed safer. Richard obviously knew his way around the computer considering how he was able to make everything I saw magically disappear but either he didn't know about cookies or didn't think I did. Not a single word was exchanged when Richard dropped me off at the house and roared off. The second I was through the door I called the Mobile Tech Squad. They said they'd be at the house within 15 minutes. Then I started scrambling, gathering keys to the safe, making copies of old tax returns... I wasn't sure why I felt driven to be doing what I was doing, but had no time to question my behavior. Then I realized, these were things I knew Richard could use against me, or at the least, to blackmail me.

6:30 p.m.

The Mobile Tech Squad arrived and got to work while I paced nervously in front of the living room window. It was Richard's poker night and he wouldn't be home until at least 9:30 but I was worried something would bring him back earlier. Within 30 minutes the Mobile Tech Squad packed their gear and were back out the door. Kathy called to inform me the files were uploading to her computer as we spoke. I looked at the clock. 8:45. I took two Motrin, gathered my pillow and some blankets and headed to the guest room. I wouldn't be sharing a bed with Richard tonight. In fact I wasn't sure if I ever would again.

I locked the door and prayed to be asleep before Richard got home. I knew he wouldn't come looking for me since I'd often gone to the guest bedroom following one of our tiffs, but tonight felt different and I quietly slipped a chair under the door knob just in case the lock didn't keep him out. My sleep was haunted by Richard watching me from the

shadows while I undressed, while I showered, while the masseuse he hired to come to our hotel room rubbed oil over my naked body. One scene blurred into the next. We would go to a new restaurant and he'd have me sit alone at the bar while he watched to see how long it would take someone to hit on me... Watching. He was always watching.

Chapter Four
February 26, 2010

I woke with dark circles rimming bloodshot eyes, realizing with a groan that I hadn't prepared the kids reading packets that they needed for today. I considered calling in a substitute but what would I do. Stay home? Richard was in the kitchen doing his morning routine. We passed each other wordlessly pouring coffee, pulling out bowls, returning juice the fridge, rinsing mugs and setting them in the drainer. Finally I grabbed my keys, sweater and student folders and left without a goodbye.

10:30 a.m.

Halfway through the morning I got a text from Kathy. "Can I bring some things to show you?" I replied, "Sure," I texted back. "Come at lunch."

As I lined up the kids to walk to the cafeteria I saw Kathy walking down the stairs toward me.

"My room's unlocked. I'll meet you there." She had a stack of papers in her hand.

I hurried the kids to the cafeteria and rushed back to my room. "What?" I asked.

"Luanna, it's not just pornography. There are 1600 pages of websites with pornography and prostitution and I barely tapped into the activity. You need to run, not walk, from this man as fast as you can."

In hindsight I think I went into shock.

"Do you want me to help you?" Kathy asked.

"Yes, I need help. I don't know what to do."

Kathy left as the kids filtered back into the classroom. I needed to get through the school day, parents were coming in for an art lesson. I had to pull it together. I was panicked and felt sick. Kathy turned to me and said, "Call your marriage counselor and see if you can get an emergency appointment," and walked out of the room.

I called Dr. Heard and he got me in for an emergency 15 minute session at 3:00. I walked in holding the pages that Kathy had given me. "This is just a fraction of what was on the computer," I said.

"Wow." I couldn't tell if he was surprised or impressed. He went to his desk, opened the drawer and handed me a card. It was for an attorney.

"She's reasonable and she's good. I think this is the direction you need to go. He hoodwinked us all."

I look at the card in my hand and thought, *I don't want a divorce!* I don't *want* a divorce, but maybe I need to be thinking about this. I need to get away. It was overwhelming. I went home and Richard is waiting for me.

"Do you want to go for soup?" It was Friday and we always went to a local restaurant famous for their homemade chicken soup. Are you *kidding* me? Chicken soup was the furthest thing from my mind, then I realized Richard had no idea that I had the printouts *or* that I saw Dr. Heard who just suggested I see a divorce attorney. I couldn't play my hand until it was the right time, and I couldn't think of a reason to not go fast enough.

"Ummm, okay." Dinner was strained and grueling. Trying to act "normal" was making me physically ill and I couldn't do it anymore. When we got back to the house I said, "I think you need to move to the guest room." Richard looked at me, surprised.

"This is nothing I've said… nothing I've done. This is *all* on you." He just stared at me. Throughout our entire marriage anytime we argued *I* was the one who would go to the guest bedroom. Not anymore. This was the first of many firsts to come.

Richard took his things and left the bedroom. I crawled into bed, alone.

"Dear God, what am I going to do?"

Saturday morning I woke up and went out to the kitchen. Richard was already sitting at the table with his coffee.

"You know they're having an open house at a new housing development in Carlsbad today. I think we should go look." Was he really acting as if nothing at all was wrong? That he hadn't spent the night in the guest room? That our marriage was in a precarious place?

"I have report cards to do."

"You do understand we have to be out of this house, right Luanna? We need a place to live. I think we need to at least go look at these."

The 17th day of our home in escrow would have been February 23. We needed to be prepared to move. Things were moving forward despite the fact that my world was spinning out of control.

Richard and I left to see the Carlsbad house in the pouring rain. We barely spoke on the drive to the coast. Once there we did a walk through and the realtor, who took our picture said, "Wow, for the dream home of your retirement you don't look very happy." My life was upside down and I didn't want to buy a new house. I didn't even know if Richard and I would continue having a life together. I needed time to think.

When we walked back to the realtor's office Richard was very eager to put a deal together and wanted to leave a deposit. "She wants this model by the park," he said enthusiastically to Karen. He was buying a *dream house for his wife.* Meanwhile I'd been looking at ring on Karen's finger. It spelled out the word, "Faith." When Richard excused himself to go to the restroom I said, "You are a woman of faith," nodding at her hand, "and you need to know I've just opened Pandora's box. *Please,* don't cash that check. I don't know what's going on but I promise I will be in contact with you." Richard returned and Karen acted as if I never said a word, going along with all of Richard's suggestions, remaining polite and friendly. That's when I realized complete strangers were being put in my path to help me. Women help women. True, they could be your worst enemy, but when needed they will rally.

We drove home in torrential rain. I have a favorite Christian radio station I listen to in the car and a song came on, "The eye of the storm," and I realized how God was holding me, keeping me afloat. I was truly in the eye of the storm and I just had to hold on to Christ because I would never survive this alone.

When we got home I started working on the computer again because I had to do report cards. Richard was at his desk doing some book work and I said, "Richard, do you know what cookies are?" He always stood up when answering a question. "Cookies? What do you mean?"

"Do you know what cookies are on the computer?"

"Well, yes, do *you* know what cookies are on the computer?"

"As a matter of fact I do. That's where all the information is stored on the computer." I looked at him. "Because of cookies nothing is *ever* removed, even if it's scrubbed clean." Richard had a look on his face that I'd never seen before. He started to talk then stopped.

"So are you going to pony up?"

"What do you mean?"

"Well, you blamed Ross for what I found on the computer and it *clearly* wasn't Ross. It's you Richard."

I paused allowing my words to sink in.

"I want six months of bank records," I said.

"What? Why?"

"Because I want to see where our money's going. Or where our money has gone. I know there's a lot of money missing. I'm working two jobs and we can't make ends meet. *Really?* I also want six months of phone records."

"No."

"No? Then I'll get them. Why don't you just tell me what I'm going to see?"

He thought about it and said, "OK, Luanna, I would find it entertaining when you would go to work I would go on the Internet and look at women and call and inquire about their donation."

"*Donation?* What does that even mean?"

"Well, what they charge."

"What they charge for their services?" I was trying to understand.

"I found it entertaining to call them and just ask them about the donation."

"After viewing them on the Internet?"

"Yes."

"Richard, why don't you just tell me everything?"

"I am."

"I don't know what questions to ask or even how to ask them so I am asking you… no… I'm *begging* you to tell me the truth. I want you to tell me the truth because you think you scrubbed the computer clean because there are things on there you don't want me to see."

"I told you everything there is to tell."

"Have you cheated on me?"

He paused. "Well…"

"Have you been with another woman since we've been married?"

He paused then said, "Maybe 10 or 11 times."

"*Maybe* 10 or 11 times? What does that mean? Like once a year? Maybe on your birthday?…"

"Richard you need to know that I'm going to look at the phone records. I want to know how long and how often you're doing this."

"Well, I do it every day when you go to work."

"Every day? And how much time do you spend every day?"

"A couple hours."

"Really." It was a statement, not a question.

I was stunned and knew it was time to stop. While he was admitting to *some* things I knew he was far from telling the truth. As soon as he said, "10 or 11 times" I was stunned into silence and shocked. I wasn't sure what I expected if I expected any number at all, so I stopped. I returned to report cards and Richard went back to the books he was working on, but I couldn't focus. My mind was playing one potential disaster after another. I felt panicked wondering what Richard could or would use against me when he realized that I found him out. *The photos,* was the first thing that came to mind. I had to get those photos. On my 40th birthday Richard's *gift to me* was having a photographer take "boudoir" photos. Of course I now know that they weren't for me at all. Although tastefully done the photos were kept under lock and key in our safe. There was no telling how Richard would lash back after I exposed him. I went to the safe, took the photos and retreated to the bedroom. Sitting on the floor inside my close, I called my "ya -ya sister," Julie.

"I need to tell you a little story," I said when she answered. " I'm actually calling you from inside my closet." While I filled her in I tore the photos into tiny pieces.
"Oh my God, Luanna…" Julie had been cheated on and been through her own divorce. She quickly started telling me things I needed to do. "Make sure you get keys to everything, including

the spares," she said. "Start putting things in your car and to take the spare keys."

I took the torn pictures downstairs and walked past Richard to the back yard. "I'm burning these," I said passing him. He said, "The lighter's right here and I already cleaned out the fire pit. I knew you would do this." He always let me know that he knew my every move and was always one step ahead of me. I stood and watched as every single photo curled and burned until there was nothing left but cold, grey ash.

I went to bed. From that night on I locked the door and kept a chair underneath the knob. Sunday morning I got up and continued working on report cards. There was no way I could work tomorrow. I had too much to do. I had to get to the bank, meet with our investment guy… I called for a sub and returned to the business at hand with a new sense of resolve. Tomorrow would be a busy day.

Chapter Seven

February 29, 2010

I walked into the bank hoping to meet with the manager. Gabby and I have known each other for years and she seemed surprised to see me on a Monday morning. She asked if one of her new employees could sit in. I was surprised to see one of our former babysitters. I liked Carol and said it was fine with me but that my news was somewhat disturbing. After sharing what I found they seemed to understand the urgency of wanting to expedite bank records. From the bank I went to see our investment consultant who told me Richard had been moving money between accounts for years, and had even signed my name on many documents. Nothing was surprising me anymore.

It seemed like months instead of days since Kathy brought me the papers she printed out from the cookies. Since then she'd been researching "spyware" I could install on our home computer. Richard said he would stop his daily phone calls to prostitutes and I wanted to see if he was. Kathy suggested a spyware that had been recommended by both Oprah and Dr. Phil. I installed the spyware that day. Every time Richard went on the computer Kathy's computer would spring to life, recording every key stroke Richard typed. Installing that software was the best thing I could have done.

Chapter Eight

March 4, 2010

I decided I needed to change passwords on our investment accounts. Ross's college fund was part of the trust left to me from my parents. Had Richard tapped into that account as well? What about my Roth (retirement) account and my Teacher's Shelter Annuity? I will be forever grateful to Mike for walking me through everything I needed to know beginning with the very basics. As I changed passwords, Kathy watched Richard's activity on the computer, seeing his frustration when he was denied access to my personal accounts. Of course he could never bring this up with me because that would be an admission that he'd been tapping into my trust fund and Ross's college fund, forging my name on money transfers and cash withdrawals.

Every night when I would go to bed I would find a note on the nightstand from Richard. "Please read this passage and we'll pray together at 6:00," he said. Of course 6:00 came and went without me. Richard began using my faith against me. *Why was I unable to be forgiving? If I was truly a Christian I would be able to move past his "minor indiscretions."* Richard would highlight passages in books he wanted me to read. He started using God to manipulate me which made my resentment toward him grow.

The more Richard pushed me to "talk" the more I withdrew. We needed to resolve issues with the sale of our house that closed escrow in April and make decisions on the new house in Carlsbad. There was always a sense of urgency with Richard and when I stopped saying, "How high" when he said, "jump" he became increasingly angry. It *appeared* that he was honoring his promise to not use our home computer to solicit prostitutes, but Kathy and I suspected he was using a disposable phone. As if the intensity of dealing with our personal lives and the properties weren't enough Richard and I were also meeting with Dr. Heard to sign papers and work on "de-coupling." I went back to my divorce attorney and had my living trust rewritten. If something happened to me I wanted everything to go to the kids. Then I changed my will. I was leaving nothing to chance.

Chapter Nine

March 5, 2010

I called another substitute teacher to take my class for the day. Ross was coming home and I had a lot to do. Richard was still sleeping in the guest room and I wasn't willing to have him back in our bedroom for "appearances sake." The kids were used to us not talking for long periods of time after one of our spats, but they never saw us in separate bedrooms. The separation wasn't lost on Ross.

"What's going on?" he asked when he saw the rumpled bed in the guest room and Richard's clothes on the back of the chair.

"Talk to dad. We're having some trouble." There was tremendous tension in the house but it was never addressed and to this day I still don't know if Ross talked to Richard or not.

When Ross went back to school I went back to the attorney. *What would be mine from the sale of the house? How did I get my share?* I had a growing stack of bank statements, past and current. I'd obtained as many phone records as I could get. Since I had absolutely no working knowledge of our finances in our 20-plus years of marriage I was learning as much as I could as quickly as I could. I wanted to find out if we'd been delinquent on bills and if my credit had been affected. As promised, I called Karen and told her to move forward with the purchase of the Carlsbad house, but under the condition that it was in my name only. If I couldn't qualify for the loan then I didn't want the house. The condo that Jill and Billy were living in was mine, purchased with funds my mom left me when she died. I hoped it would be enough to qualify for the loan, but Jill and Billy began pushing me to sign the property over to them, creating yet more tension within the family. I knew Richard and Billy had been meeting and my paranoia grew. I began avoiding calls from Jill and Billy when I knew it was about the condo. I was trying to stay one step ahead of Richard and, thanks to the spyware, I was. I knew when he was trying to get into accounts and when he was trying to access funds. He wasn't willing to let me see the Visa bill which I suspected was being used to pay for his extra curricular activities. Since it was in his name only there was no way for me to access the information. We were expecting a $10,000 tax return check. When it arrived Richard forged my name on the check and paid off his Visa bill. *How could this have happened?* I called our tax man and he hung up on me. Richard had gotten to him, and people were afraid to cross Richard.

Chapter Ten

March 23-31, 2010

Text messages from Richard

March 23, 2010

3:46 p.m.

please give me another chance to love you and to make our family whole again. God has forgiven me and he has covered my sins with his love. I am asking from the heart to come back and be a godly loving caring devoted husband and father. I am so very sorry that I hurt you. I love you and I need the chance to finally show you please search your heart for me   Richard

3:48 p.m.

please know that I have been in sincere and honest prayer with God to save our marriage to have him release me from the bondage of the devil   please take a few minutes to read the first pages of a book I have started and would like to share with you. I love you.

March 25, 2010

6:25 p.m.

Everything will be done as you want please be patient
put your faith in God through prayer and He will help
us and bring us peace and healing I Love You.

March 30, 2010

3:05 p.m.

I now know Luanna that your greatest need is for
affection please give me another chance to show you
newer affection in our marriage please pray at least
twice a day for our marriage and acknowledge God in
everything you do. I Love You.

March 31, 2010

7:59 p.m.

I Love You I am praying hard for us and our marriage.

Chapter Eleven

April 1, 2010

"When are you moving out?" I asked Richard grabbing my purse and keys, heading out the door for school.

"When you see my stuff gone you'll know I'm out." It was the most we'd said to each other in weeks. I'd been trying to stay away from the house. I wanted Richard gone, and then a harsh reality set in. Where was *I* going to live? The new owners were moving in the end of April. Our finances were so tied up I wasn't sure what I would do. And then, once again, it was like an angel of God opened a door for me. The parent of a child stopped in my classroom after school and asked if we needed a place to live until the Carlsbad house was built. Ten minutes after she made the offer I called her. I knew the woman only through her child, my student, but it was becoming easier to open up to complete strangers, something I never would have done before. "I don't know what to do," I said when she answered the phone, and one more time, my story began to pour out. "I'm scared and need a place to live... but I can't pay you."

"Bring a few of your things and come see the house in Coronado over spring break." *The house was perfect.* "Where are you going to store your things?" *My God I'd never thought about it.* "I have no idea."

"No worries," she said. She had a big storage unit and said I could put all my things there until I decided what I wanted to do. Just like that, I had a place to live, I didn't have to pay storage or rent, only for the movers. I told Richard when he left to take whatever he wanted. I realized this was truly the beginning of the end.

Chapter Twelve

April 5-April 9, 2010

The kids still didn't know their father and I were splitting up. Richard and I agreed that we would have a family meeting when Ross got home from school at the end of the month. So much needed to be done that I lost track of days and hours, moving robotically between school, packing the house, picking and choosing and preparing a new house. It became overwhelming. I had to do a "walk through" with the new owners April 19th and be moved out by the 23rd. With my world crumbling down around me I found it hard to even think about what granite I wanted in the kitchen or whether to select door handles or door knobs for the bathroom. Meanwhile, I continued taking crash courses on how to pay bills on line. That night I dreamed of teaching in Australia.

April 6, 2010

7:45 p.m.

I pray that you prayed for our marriage today. I Love you.

April 9, 2010

There's no shortage of Mexican eateries in southern California and I'm fortunate that one of the best is a stone's throw from my school. I decided after a very long, emotional day, that a burrito and a beer was just what the doctor ordered.

I brought my burrito and beer home, kicked off my shoes and sat down to eat in the living room while I watched the news. Then I realized I was staring at a bare wall. *The television was gone; so was Richard.* He said I'd know he was gone when his stuff was gone.

He was gone. Surprisingly, it scared, more than comforted me.

April 9, 2010

Text message from Richard

I pray desperately for a new beginning for our marriage. I Love You.

April 10, 2010

6:41 p.m.

Luanna, I am truly sorry that I have hurt you so deeply. I Love You.

Chapter Thirteen

April 11, 2010

It was Easter Sunday, and we were expected at Jill and Billy's. When I arrived Richard was already there. Everyone stopped talking when I walked in and I could tell from Jill's expression that she is furious.

"Why do you have to be so mean to dad?" she finally said, glaring at me. *"Why are you so mean?"* I wonder exactly how much, or *what,* Richard has been saying to her and Billy but I didn't want to go there. Not today.

"I am not being mean, Jill," I said, trying to sound nonchalant. The tension in the house was palpable. Then, quite literally, the earth shook. *Earthquake.* I grabbed Jill's dogs and ran outside until the rumbling stopped then went back for the dog's leashes.

Richard must have decided it was time for him to leave. He'd gathered his things and I could tell he'd been crying.

"I'm taking the dogs for a walk," I said to no one in particular, closing the door behind me. When I return Jill is *enraged.*

"You... are... so... mean." Her words were measured and cruel.

"Really?"

Richard and I agreed not to talk to the kids about our separation until everyone was together. Ross would be back home in a matter of weeks, but this had gotten out of control and I'd had enough.

"Jill, your dad has spent our life savings on prostitution," I was so angry my voice was shaking. "He's deceived me for the past 25 years. He has spent hundreds of *thousands* of dollars on prostitutes and *I* ... *never* ... *knew*. I've been tested for HIV, for every type of sexually transmitted disease... " Billy was looking at me, shocked. I ignored the look he was sending my way.

"So don't you *dare* tell me I'm being mean to your dad. I pray to God that you *never, ever* have done to you what's been done to me."

Billy cleared his throat and broke the silence. "I think you're being a bit too descriptive Luanna. You *are* talking to your daughter."

That was it. I was done here. "I love you Jill with all my heart, but when you think *I've* done all of this to your dad, you're not seeing the big picture." She kept her head down on the kitchen table and continued sobbing as I turned and walked out the door. There was going to be hell to pay for my outburst and I knew it.

Text message from Richard:

Praying for our marriage and our family.

Chapter Fourteen

April 15, 2010

It was our weekly session with Dr. Heard. When I arrived, Richard was already there. I knew before closing the door that he was furious. Richard stood and turned toward me before I even took my seat next to the counselor. Richard was literally shaking from head to toe, pointing at me.

"She betrayed me... as bad or worse than I have betrayed her," he spat the words. Dr. Heard tried diffusing the situation. "How did she do that Richard?" he asked.

"*She told Jill,*" he said, "when we agreed *not* to tell the kids until *I* could talk to them." Was that what he was upset about? That *he needed to be in control of how and what was said?* That *he* needed to be in control of not only what was said but what they *heard*?

He truly believed I wronged him. The slight bit of guilt I felt for telling Jill on Easter vanished when I found out it was Billy who told Richard what had happened the following day when they met for breakfast. Apparently they'd been meeting regularly to discuss ways to get me to sign over the condo to Jill and Billy. I couldn't help but think Richard had some ulterior motive for trying help the "kids" get the property from me.

After my disclosure to Jill I think it finally sunk in with Richard that it was over, so he began trying to make me realize how much I needed him. *I didn't want to do this. I needed his income.* He didn't want to hear that I had a place to live. My friends and co-workers were holding me up emotionally. God was holding me up spiritually.

Text messages from Richard:

April 16th

8:28 p.m

Good Night Luanna I Love You

April 17th

8:10 p.m.

I miss you lots Luanna I Love you Goodnight

April 18th

7:41 p.m.

Thanks for the time. I just want a chance when you are ready to show you how much I love you.

April 20th

I love you Luanna. I hope your cold is better. Good
night.

April 21st

Call me

April 21st

Can I take some chicken soup home for you

April 21st

<u>*(Text message from me to Richard)*</u>*:*

No thank you

April 22nd

I love you Lu Good Night

April 23rd

I love you Good Night

Chapter Fifteen

April 24, 2010

It's moving day. Richard shows up at the storage facility to make sure I pay the movers so he wouldn't get the bill. The day is riddled with tension. Another chapter of my life is ending. When I finally got to the Coronado house I crawled into bed. Minutes later I received a text message from Richard.

7:47 p.m.

```
Lu Thanks for the nice day I really appreciated being
with you today I  Love You goodnight
```

Are you kidding? Richard couldn't possibly think this day, with its somber finality and not a word spoken between us, was a *nice day?* I didn't respond, but my silence didn't deter his continued messaging.

April 25th

7:51 p.m.

```
I Love You good Night Lu
```

April 26th

9:10 a.m.

`Call me.`

April 26th

8:29 p.m.

`Good night Lu I Love You`

April 29th

11:35 a.m.

`Please call`

That afternoon I met Richard in the park behind the school to get some papers from him. I no longer felt safe meeting him in private.

April 29th

7:56 p.m.

Nice seeing you today Luanna. I miss you very much
Good night I love you

April 30th

8:11 p.m.

Miss you very much Lu Please pray for our marriage and
family Good night I Love You Please give me another
chance I am so sorry for what I did to you and the
terrible pain I caused you. I will truly be remorseful
for the rest of my life.

Chapter Sixteen

May 1 - May 16, 2010

Text messages from Richard:

May 1st

11:28 a.m

Good morning Lu. I miss you.

May 1st

7:50 p.m

I'm sorry Good Night I Love You Please pray for our marriage and family

May 2

10:34 a.m.

Do you have time for a cup of coffee today and little conversation?

May 3, 2010

4 p.m.

I was meeting with my new therapist to talk about a divorce. In my mind I felt like we were talking about a death. There was little difference.

"All I wanted was for him to tell me the truth," I kept saying over and over. "I gave him every opportunity but he... couldn't. He didn't know I could see every single thing he was doing because of the spyware. I gave him every chance to be honest with me. He just couldn't stop lying." Dr. Hancock's role was to help guide me through this new season of my life ... a life without Richard. I went from her office to my attorney's office and rewrote my living trust.

Text message from Richard:

May 9, 2010

7:51 p.m.

```
Hope you had a nice day I love you and miss you
```

As the legal wrangling began so did my withdrawal. I had no television in the Coronado house and didn't want any. Friends gave me hundreds of DVD's that I'd watch long into the night and early morning. I stopped going to church. I was so humiliated I didn't want to be seen. Every day I continued to do a daily devotional. It was how I coped. Weeks passed.

Chapter Seventeen

May 16, 2010

It's Jill's 25th birthday. In my family when you turned 25 it was a very big deal, so I wanted it to be a special day for her, despite all that we were going through. When I turned 25 I received a one-carat diamond pendant from my parents that I gave to Jill when she got married. Richard gave me diamond earrings one year for my birthday. I decided to give her the earrings for her 25th birthday to match. She would love them, and I no longer wanted them.

Jill had lunch with Richard, and dinner with me. Since the disaster of Easter my relationship with Jill and Billy was even more strained. Ross would be home on the 20th and still didn't know his father and I were separating. He would turn 21 in eight days and I wanted to do something special for him so arranged for he and a couple of friends to go to Las Vegas. The family meeting was scheduled for the day after his return. May 26.

Chapter Eighteen

May 26, 2010

George's at the Cove is located in the pristine area of La Jolla, California. With rooftop dining and sweeping views of the ocean it's a popular spot with locals and tourists alike. Richard wasn't pleased that I wanted to meet in a public place but I told him it wasn't his choice. A public place would assure things wouldn't spiral out of control and that, hopefully, there wouldn't be a scene.

Since Ross came back from school he'd been staying with me at the house I was "borrowing" in Coronado. He knew the Park Ranch house had sold and we were waiting for the Carlsbad house to be finished but didn't ask why his dad and I weren't staying in the same place. I had to wonder if he'd talked to Jill after Easter. I knew Jill and Billy were prepared for what was to come. I had a sense that Ross knew there was something serious going on.

Because of the spyware I knew *everything* Richard was preparing to say. He'd typed a letter he planned to read at the meeting that, of course, Kathy saw and printed out so I could be "prepared." Before our meeting I told Richard that he couldn't say things like "a few" or "a couple" that would minimize his infidelities because I would call him on it. He couldn't say I hadn't given him fair warning.

We were taken to our table and Billy ordered drinks for everyone. When the waitress returned with our order Richard snapped at her, telling her not to bother us again. I cringed at his rudeness.

In true fashion, Richard stood when he was ready to address the kids and said he wanted to tell them the reason we were separating. He pulled the letter from his pocket and said he would "allow" questions when he was finished but did *not* want to be interrupted.

"The purpose of this meeting," he began, *"Is to tell you the reason why Mother and I have separated.*

I will give you a summary.

As you know we have been in and out of marriage and family counseling for most of our marriage. We have currently been seeing Dr. Heard for the past couple of years and since our separation, he has directed us to individual counselors. Both Dr. Heard and my counselor have advised us that you are entitled to know the reason for the separation but many of the intimate details will be kept personal between your Mother and me. My counselor agrees with Dr. Heard's observation.

This will be a summary of the situation and this meeting should not be considered to be the "all or end all" as I will be willing to answer any appropriate questions afterwards or in the future by meeting with the two of you, together or individually.

Please listen carefully with an open mind.

In late February, Mother came home from work and went onto Ross's computer upstairs — I was in the kitchen. She came downstairs and asked me to look at something on the computer. She showed me the various sexually explicit Craigslist sites that were displayed and advertised for various services. Mother asked me if I knew anything about this and my immediate reaction was to lie and say that I did not. This then deflected the Confession Statement blame back to Ross even though neither one of us knew if this was technically possible. I held on to this lie and denial through the next day. After work the next day, Mother confronted me with the fact that it was not technically possible for Ross to have been on these web sites. I then confessed to her that it was all my doing.

Ross, I owe you an apology, for my disgusting lack of judgment and trying to implicate you in my appalling behavior — I pray that one day you will be able to forgive me.

Not only did I confess to Mother that the sites she saw was all my doing, but that I routinely went on the Craigslist sites and other porn sites — I guess I had convinced myself that this was a form of sick entertainment for me. Even though I called some of these sites, and some on a daily basis… I never acted on any of them or followed up — I had a very curious attraction for lack of better terms.

My other transgression or moral lapse started approximately 12 years ago shortly before Mother's 40th birthday. To the best of my recall, the activity with Craigslist and the other sites was within the last 18-24 months and continued up to approximately one year ago. It happened over an infrequent time frame (7 or 8 times) period.

I went to massage parlors, sinned against our marriage and your Mother by going. In retrospect, these actions were horrific shocking and sad behaviors are totally my fault and responsibility. I had choices to make and I failed in my responsibilities to my wife, my marriage, and to my family, and to my children. I am deeply sorry and full of regret and shame for the hurt and sorrow that I have caused my family just to seek gratification. I love you guys.

Jill and Ross, I apologize to you sincerely for my failures, and pain. Luanna, no words can express my remorsefulness for the wrong I have committed against you. I love you guys."

He then decided to share a previous letter he had written and read to me at our therapist's office on April 1st.

Luanna,

Please give me another chance to show you that I can unconditionally love you and give you the affection, and kindness that you deserve. Through God's grace, I know now that I am capable of devoting my life to you as a caring and understand husband and father. I have been open to allowing God to change and restore me, and through prayer God is giving me a pure mind, free of temptation, along with a loving and patient heart.

Please don't allow our separation to destroy our marriage. Nothing in this life means more to me than you, Jill and Ross — our family.

Through God's love and continual prayer we can heal, renew our marriage, save our Family and live for the purpose God has intended for us.

We are capable of having many wonderful, loving, caring years together. I want nothing more than to be with you in the years ahead. To work and play as one in our marriage. To be a dedicated husband — to understand every facet of your life — to accept you, your need and desires — to embrace you - to see you for who you truly are Luanna - to listen to you -to hear you- to communicate well with you — to touch you —to talk with you (yes, I have set aside my foolish sin of pride and can finally see and hear with a clear pure mind) - to be in your essence - to smell your essence - to pray with you — to pray for us — to pray for our family — to be there for Jill and Ross and perhaps our grandchildren — to live a spiritual life — to make all of our decisions together as a couple — to stop the separateness — to restore your dreams of early retirement and travel — to set *priorities — to cast out fear in our love — to build trust — to un-clutter and to live a simple life - to be there for you in sickness and in health and always.*

As the years pass we will strengthen our marriage bond, commitment, and love. We will know that we have persevered through evil and hurt and found peace through God's Grace. Prayer works!

Luanna, I am so remorseful for my wronging and the pain I have caused you. I sincerely apologize to you.

.... PLEASE, PLEASE, find it in your heart to give me another chance. Please don't give up on our marriage — our Family — on me.

I LOVE YOU!

P.S. Please know that I have asked Jill and Ross to pray for us.

Richard concluded by telling Jill and Ross that he'd written me many letters apologizing, but I was unwilling to forgive him, and if I was *truly* a Christian woman, I *would* be able to forgive him. Surprisingly, I felt an unexpected calm while Richard read both letters, in fact, I felt almost *peaceful*, then realized it was because God prepared me for everything I would hear.

"I ask you to pray for our marriage and for your mother to be willing to forgive me."

Richard sat back down and looked around the table. "OK …
Are there any questions?" Ross was the first to speak. *"You
broke the law,"* he said, surprising me. It wasn't what I expected,
but I guess with Ross being a criminal justice major, it was the
first thing that came to mind. *"I can't believe you broke the
law,"* he sounded … shocked.

"Not really," Richard said looking at Ross as if he had no
idea what his son was talking about. *"I didn't really do anything
that would be harmful to your mother physically."* I was
stunned. Stunned and *seething.* Did Richard really believe
prostitution wasn't against the law. Ross called him a "John" and
then said, "Dad, I forgive you. I just hope Christ will forgive
you." Jill, who started crying when Richard stood to read,
continued sobbing, asking over and over, "Why would you do
that? Why?" Richard gave her no answer.

After a few moments I said, "Can I speak now?" Richard
whipped his head in my direction. "I don't want you to speak.
This is *not your meeting.*" Any other time I would have shrunk
back. *Not today.*

"Well, it's a *family* meeting and I have the facts," I said
looking at him without hesitation. He obviously didn't believe
me when I told him I would call him on minimizing his
infidelities.

"You missed a word when you said you had "seven or eight" indiscretions, I said returning his glare. "You omitted the word *hundred.*" I opened the folder I'd been holding on my lap. The kids looked at me…. stunned. I turned away from Richard and spoke to them directly.

"I have documentation from a private investigator that I hired that shows your father has had hundreds, *hundreds,* of encounters with prostitutes, not just *seven or eight* as he would like you to believe." I looked at Richard and could see he was seething but I was not to be deterred. He had no idea, until this moment, that I'd hired a private investigator.

Despite the fact that we were in a very public, very upscale place, Richard was unable to contain his rage.

"How dare you? *How dare you?*" he said, visibly shaking. I have *not* done that," he looked at his children for support but they were expressionless.

"You've deceived me our whole life." My voice was barely a whisper, yet very calm and measured. "This meeting is adjourned."

Ross stood first, coming to my side of the table, and put his arm around me. Jill and Billy immediately went to Richard. There was a visible divide of allegiances. The ugly truth was out. I decided to let the Holy Spirit take it from here. Ross and I headed for the parking lot, Richard, Jill and Billy for the bar. To this day I don't know what they talked about.

Friday, May 28, 2010

4 p.m.

This would be our last meeting with Dr. Heard. *Another door closes,* I thought. *Another chapter coming to an end.* When I arrived Richard was already there. He was pacing and seemed distraught. I had to wonder if it was because I called him out in front of both of his kids and son-in-law. Richard was never able to admit to any fault and continued to blame the demise of our marriage on my unwillingness to perform my "wifely duties." Our session was horrible. I could tell Richard was trying to devise a plan and I had no idea what it was.

Richard began texting me almost every day. "Goodnight Lu. I love you." Another: "I missed you so much today." I felt strong but hard-hearted and I knew that wasn't coming from God or the Holy Spirit, it was from years of neglect. Some of the messages ran a cold chill down my spine: "I know, Luanna, that your greatest need is for affection. Please pray at least twice a day for our marriage." He really wasn't getting it.

Kathy checked the printout daily that continued uploading to her computer from the installed spyware. She told me Richard was trying to expedite a new passport to leave the country. She said he'd been doing extensive research on Indonesia. I knew he went to Mexico with a retired police officer because he shared the excursion with Ross. Something shared in the conversation that Ross had with Jill had her scared that Richard, with the help of his retired police officer friend, was looking for a hit man. I had my living trust in order, and I no longer felt afraid. Maybe, as my friends insisted, I was still in shock. There seemed to be a great need for them to *protect* me. But I no longer felt the fear.

Tuesday, June 1st

When Richard was confronted with the data the private investigator gleaned from our personal computer he promised to stop "hunting" for prostitutes online. Activity came virtually to a standstill with the spyware showing no visits to any of the porn sites he'd been frequenting. Kathy and I suspected, however, that he was using a disposable phone for his activities which were, literally, untraceable.

Then, on June 1st, the spyware sprung to life as Richard's sexual addiction took hold. Whether it was the realization that our marriage was truly over, or the realization that his sexual addiction had been discovered and exposed, Richard seemed to be spiraling out of control. For *18 hours* he never left his computer. At times his searching seemed frenetic. Kathy alerted me when the activity began and from her computer we watched as Richard desperately tried to find the contact information for one of his favorite prostitutes, but couldn't remember her name. He typed every variation of every name that began with the letter *S*. Thanks to the 1600-plus pages of activity that Kathy printed out in February, we were able to cross-reference each prostitute's phone number to learn her name and address, then confirm her "donation" with the amount withdrawn from an

ATM closest to the hooker's location. We watched as he frantically tried to find Sadie, his favorite, $500-an-hour, 50-year-old hooker. The real Richard was back, stripped of the contrite, often teary, apologetic, husband and father he tried to purport since being found out. The man I'd been married to for 25 years was back, still not knowing that I was seeing every single thing he was doing online.

Chapter Eighteen

Cellphone logs

June 9, 2010

6:51 a.m.

Text message from Richard:

I asked for a meeting yesterday. You did not respond.
I will ask one more time for a time and a place. No
excuses, no stalling. YOU NOW HAVE MY ATTENTION.

Text message from me to Richard

12:17 p.m.

I don't understand why there is urgency? Please allow
me to focus on my career and finish up my school year.

1:22 p.m.

Reply from Richard:

We need to talk today before you go home.

2:28 p.m.

Text message from Ross:

Hey mom you going to Coronado after work?

2:28 p.m.

Text message from Richard

Meet you in the park after school. What time are you available?

3:03 p.m.

Text message from Richard:

I'm in the park waiting for your answer.

3:52 p.m.

Text message from me to Ross:

Yes, I will b n Coronado later.

3:55 p.m.

Text message from Ross:

Alright. I am down here now. Spencer just got here.

4:08 p.m.

Text from me to Ross

Ok, have fun c ya

6:48 p.m.

Voice message from Richard:

.

"Hope your busy day is about to end. I'm a little bit saddened that I couldn't steal you away for a couple of minutes today but I guess thats the nature of the beast these days. I did have a couple of questions I wanted to ask you but I guess I'm not going to get those answered either, so I thought I'd try just one last time tonight to see if you were available but I guess you're not … you're not picking up, so my questions can go unanswered. Talk to you later, bye."

*   *   *

Jill and Billy upped the ante to get me to sign over the condo to them by saying Billy's family was willing to put up the money to buy the condo out from under me. Something kept telling me, "Don't sign those papers." I was being pushed hard; hard from Jill, hard from Richard, hard from Billy. Jill's calls and texts about signing the papers escalated, but I kept ignoring them. Richard and Billy's meetings, phone conversations and texts seemed more frequent. I was getting paranoid. It seemed like Richard was getting the kids to gang up on me when all I was doing was trying to keep what was mine.

In addition to the texts and voice messages of June 9th, there were an additional 38 phone calls and texts between Richard, Ross, Billy and Jill that I wasn't a part of. To this day I don't know what those calls and texts were about… all I knew was that Richard's last text left me feeling unsettled. His day began at 6:52 a.m. with a call to Ross. By the time I finished listening to his last message at 6:48 I felt like I needed to get out of the Coronado house to safer waters. I didn't know if this heightened feeling of unease came from the stress the school year ending, physical, mental and emotional exhaustion, or… unadulterated fear. When I got to Coronado, Ross was there with Spencer, but I felt like I wasn't *safe* and packed a bag to go stay with Jackie and Jeff in Escondido.

I was so saddened that I felt safe with friends, but not my own family.

June 11th

8:05 p.m.

Phone message from Jill:

Hey mom it's me, just wanted to tell you the papers (transferring ownership of the condo to Jill and Billy) are on your washing machine… and to see how you're doing. Love you. Bye.

June 12th

I was still staying at Jeff and Jackie's. I knew I needed to pack up my classroom to officially close out the school year. After more than two decades of marriage, I also knew that Richard knew what I would be doing that weekend before the school year ended.

Paranoid or not, *I was terrified I'd be hijacked while alone in my classroom.*

130

Jackie took me over to the school at 6 a.m. I didn't want my car to be recognized in the parking lot. When Jackie stopped at the curb I opened the door and ran down the stairs to my classroom, unlocked, entered, then re-locked the door once inside. I ran to the window twisting the acrylic wand to close the blinds. I felt safe inside my classroom. As an extra precaution I slipped off my shoes and tossed them near the door so if anyone stopped to listen they wouldn't hear me walking about.

Hours later I was paralyzed with the realization I hadn't planned for one contingency… needing to use the restroom which was up the stairs and across the campus. What if Richard was lurking somewhere, watching? I'd been so careful. I looked around my disassembled classroom. The cabinet doors to the art supplies stood ajar. On the second shelf were a dozen or more 32-ounce water containers with ill-fitting lids. *It'll have to do,* I thought.

"Wow… is this what 'surviving' has come to?" Without a second thought, I grabbed and used the container then snapped on the lid and secured it inside a box of things to be disposed of later that day.

Twelve hours later Jackie picked me up and we took my car where it wouldn't be found. I was leaving town for a much needed break.

I touched base with Jill and Ross before I left but didn't tell them I was going away for a few days. Quite honestly I felt the need to disappear to a place where I wouldn't have to answer emails, texts or cellphones. But before I hung up with Jill I asked, *'Do you think I'm in any physical danger?'* Jill hesitated and was silent longer than I was comfortable before answering.

"Well... I don't *think* so."

It was *not* convincing.

Tuesday, June 15, 2010

7:01 p.m.

Phone message from Jill:

"Hey mom it's me. I know you have one day left and I hope tomorrow goes well for you. If you have a chance give me a call."

7:54 p.m.

"Hi mom, I'm home now. I don't know if you got my first message. Give me a call if you can or just text me letting me know you're ok. I love you."

Chapter Nineteen

June 16, 2010

The day before what *should* have been my last day of school a friend picked me up and drove me to the airport. The stress of the past four months had taken its toll, both emotionally and physically. I'd lost more than 30 pounds. I never slept through the night and when I did it was never for more than an hour or two at a time. I had a melanoma removed from my scalp and my hair seemed to be falling out in patches. It took every ounce of sheer will and determination to finish out the school year minus one day. *I needed this escape.*

By 3:00 I was on my way to Arizona to spend a week with one of my Ya-Ya sisters. Although I texted Jill the night before I didn't tell her I was leaving for a few days. I didn't want anyone to know where I was going and didn't want to talk to anyone. All I wanted to do *was to do nothing at all;* not think, not be afraid, not have to worry about "what's next." I stopped responding to Richard's emails and texts when they became incessant and more threatening. I again began feeling less safe and more frightened. Unbeknownst to me, a firestorm would begin brewing before my plane even left the runway. I told Kathy and Jackie I was leaving for a few days and how to find me in case of a bonafide emergency, but they knew how important this little getaway was for me.

Little did I know my departure would result in a full scale, police-involved, investigation. The following morning I powered-up my phone to find a plethora of phone messages.

5:13 p.m.

Text message from Billy

Queen, we are all very concerned and want to make sure you are ok. I know you might not feel like talking, but could you text back just so we know you're ok. We have tried to contact and find you all over San Diego. I understand if you don't want anyone to know where you are. We just want you to know we love you and just want to make sure you're ok. If you could please text any of us it would lift a huge weight of deep concern for you. Love Billy, Jill and Ross.

6:31 p.m.

I replied to Billy's text with a single word:

"OK."

6:35 p.m.

Phone message from Jill:

Mom, it's me. I don't know if someone's using your phone to text... I've been to the airport looking up and down for your car, I've been to Coronado, we've been to L.R. Green, I've called Jackie, I've called every number, I've called Judy, I need to hear your voice or I'm filing a missing person report tomorrow. I took tomorrow off and I would like to see you. I don't know if you have time... Please call us. Bye."

Text message from Billy

6:36 p.m.

Thank you. If you could possibly manage to call Jill. She is in shambles as I can imagine you are. She just wants to hear your voice. We are very concerned if Jill cannot reach you for your safety. She is going to file a missing person report. We are all very concerned and love you.

Text message from Billy

7:25 p.m.

If it is an issue about monitoring phone #s, I can
block my phone number so it won't show up on any
records if this is an issue of contact I will get u a
prepaid untracked ph.

Text message from me to Jill,

7:36 p.m.

Jill, I am fine! I m fine. I m turning off my phone. Xoxoxo moma

8:50 p.m.

Phone voice message from Jill:

Hey mom, it's me again. I know your phone's off but if
you can — and call me tomorrow or call Billy tomorrow.
We need to hear your voice 'cause anyone can send a
text message. You need to contact me. I am off
tomorrow... I've taken the day off. And I will find you
to my best ability. I am extremely concerned and I

need to hear your voice or I need to see you. I'll
talk to you later. I love you.

9:07 p.m.

Message from former nanny, Jeri:

"Hello it's Jeri, it's 10:00 at night..." (Call
disconnects).

9:07 p.m.

Phone (voice) message from Jill:

"Mom, it's me again. I know you turned off your phone. I am at
a loss for words. I don't know what to say. I don't know if you
can call me from somewhere or what or call Billy. I need to talk
to you. I need to see you. I need to know you are OK. Because
right now I've lost way too much sleep over this. I need to know
that you're still breathing If you can PLEASE call me back or
meet me tomorrow. I'm taking the day off. I will take Friday off. I
have birthday plans for you. I'll take Monday off. I don't know
what you need but I'll be there for you. Please call me back.
Love you. Bye."

Text message from Richard

```
Please call Jill.
```

Text message from Richard,

I do not want a divorce. I love you very much.
Please call me.

June 17, 2010

Phone (voice) message from Richard

Hello this is Richard. I hope you get this message. It's about 8:10 Thursday morning the 17th. I need to talk to you and I wish you would call me. I'm going to brief you on what happened last night. Jill has been frantically trying to call you, and she's called all your friends and everything…(your sister) and everybody. Last night the police broke into your house and a missing person report was filed. We were all standing out in front of your house about 1:00 (a.m.) last night, Lily and Jeri and Jill and Billy and three police officers, I think I said this but they broke into your house because you weren't responding and so you need to call me so I can brief you on what's going on. We haven't talked about anything personal in four months now and so I think it's time that we have a conversation so give me a call. Again I don't even know if you're getting this message. I don't know if your phone is on or what. We need to get through this. I know that you probably know already but I filed for divorce, and the reason I did that was to stop the purchase of the Carlsbad house. We can talk about that and what we can do about that. But if you just ignore me and continue on like this then I don't know what else I can do. We need to have a conversation so that we can discuss the Carlsbad house… so we can discuss a pending divorce if I let it go thru, etc. So please give me a call. Do not ignore this because it's not going to get any better as we move forward on this thing. Maybe there are some solutions to this that we can talk about. Jill is absolutely devastated. So give me a call please. Thank you.

Text message from Richard, 8:40 a.m.

…u we need to talk. The police broke into your house last night and a missing persons report was filed. I stopped the purchase of the house and filed for divorce until we can talk. You need to talk to me for the sake of the kids and get our situation resolved. Please do not ignore me as this has the potential to only get worse. Please allow me to explain. Please call Jill and Ross and let them know you are ok. Please know that I do not want a divorce or to lose the house but you must talk with me soon. I truly love you.

*   *   *   *

I called Jill and was somewhat relieved that it went directly to voice mail. I was initially stunned by all that transpired in less than 24 hours, but then became increasingly angry. How the drama began was anyone's guess. What I couldn't understand was how quickly it escalated, then spiraled out of control. *I'd been gone less than a day.*

June 18, 2010

Text message from Richard, 9:36 a.m.

Please check your email.

E-mail from Richard:

9:36 a.m.

Lu,

Because you have refused to have a conversation regarding our personal situation for nearly four months now, I have decided to write you this email and to present a couple of proposals to you before, as you call it, "THIS MESS" becomes irreversible and the attorneys end up with all the money, which indeed they will.

First, we could save the Carlsbad house by agreeing to purchase it jointly and sharing occupancy and determining where the relationship goes at a later date.

Second, we could stop all legal proceeds against each other (divorce, etc.) which would stop the financial bleeding.

I do not expect that you will respond to this email because I don't really believe you have the individual or christian courage to do so. You have your attorney, your personal advisors, your private investigator, etc., etc., etc., that you allow to think for you and would never allow anyone to penetrate your stubbornness - I believe you would allow everything to be destroyed before you could allow yourself to be exposed to doing the right thing for our marriage and family. Oh, and I know you're thinking that you would never put anything in writing at this stage.

Well, Lu, just my final thoughts before things get ugly - just know that you have the power to get us out of this MESS and save our marriage and our family.

Also know, that it was really, really sad and pathetic watching our Daughter breakdown in front of your house Wednesday evening at 1:00 a.m. because you would not respond and a missing persons report was filed.

As always… with love,
Richard

12:02 p.m.

Richard,

This 'MESS' is ALL your doing as I have said time and time again... I will not take responsibility for the breakdown of our marriage and family. And by the way, it is already ugly...

You have continuously involved our adult children and must stop doing so in the future - it is not about them nor is it in their best interest.

I am confused about the legal proceeding statement as you are the one who started all legal actions. I just respond to them.

The marriage and family were destroyed by you long ago, according to your actions of being unfaithful. In addition to breaking EVERY wedding vow, YOU have regularly been unfaithful AND regularly paid for sexual services.

You and I both know that the missing persons report is a total sham. I texted both Jill and Billy approx. 7:15 p.m. June 16th to let them know I was fine and turning off my pone. As you also know this is all documented.

You, Richard, will live out your years knowing what you have done and have single handedly destroyed our family and marriage. From here on out please direct all communication through my attorney, NOT our children.

Heart broken,
Luanna

Reply from Richard:

Lu,

One last piece of correspondence.

You are the one responsible NOT ME. You have always been in DENIAL. **If I had a wife who knew how to take care of her husband this would never have happened.** I asked for very little in our marriage and got virtually nothing. I was in a DEAD sexless marriage for years. What I did was for YOU because you could not do it for yourself - - **you were incapable of fulfilling your wifely duties.**

The only communication we've had over the last four months was about your BUSINESS and nothing else - - all I ever heard was "I'm in survival mode." - - how pathetic!

We didn't live together for those two months, we survived (barely) together.

You were the first to demonstrate infidelity and unfaithfulness in our marriage by withholding sex - - READ THE SCRIPTURES - - how ignorant are you?

I did not initiate the missing persons report - - they stuck it in front of my face for signature and said anyone could sign the form - - Jill was too distraught.

I will live out my years knowing that I was in a DEAD MARRIAGE with a woman who was not capable of being a wife and I will always know that you were the one who destroyed our marriage and family because you were capable of nothing else.

You really need to stop telling me not to involve our adult children - - you need to give up the QUEENIE control freak stuff **- - I will always involve our children in whatever I choose to involve them in.**

I believe this responds to all of your deplorable allegations … Goodbye and thanks finally for the communication.

4:12 p.m.

Voice message from Jill:

"Hey mom it's me. Thanks for the phone call. I've cancelled everything for tomorrow, so… I'll give you a call back tomorrow just to say Happy Birthday, and I guess just contact me when you're ready. I'll be here waiting. Love you Bye."

Chapter Twenty

July 16, 2010

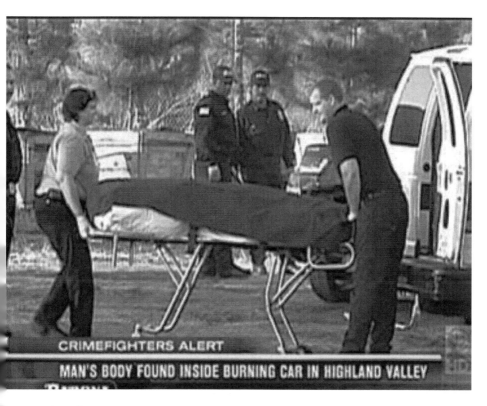

CRIMEFIGHTERS ALERT

MAN'S BODY FOUND INSIDE BURNING CAR IN HIGHLAND VALLEY

Posted: Jul 17, 2010 6:11 PM PDT

SAN DIEGO, Calif. (CBS 8) - *We still don't know the identity of a man whose body was found inside a burning car in the North County.*

It happened yesterday morning along 1400 block of Highland Valley Road in Highland Valley.
San Diego police say the man's body was discovered after firefighters put out the car fire.
Investigators say the car was not involved in an accident, and the fire may have been deliberately set.
Police also say they know who the Hyundai Sonata is registered to, but didn't reveal if it was the same man they found inside.

It was Kathy and her husband's anniversary weekend and they were hoping to get away to enjoy some time alone. After all Kathy had done for me I was happy to stay with her kids. If it wasn't for Kathy I might have never known about *cookies* or how to track someone's activity on a computer. I probably would have bought Richard's story, allowed him to smooth talk his way out of admitting guilt, talked to Ross about pornography and the dangers of Internet sex and solicitations, and went on being oblivious to the seamy, underbelly world of sexual addiction. I also don't know how I would have ever survived the months between February and now. I was still living in the house in Coronado but the Carlsbad house was done. I would enjoy living down by the beach while I move my life, piece by piece, to the coast. Although I kept telling myself I didn't want a divorce, that was the inevitable direction we were moving. Richard was either unwilling, or unable, to stop spending time and money on prostitutes. Our relationship had been irreparably damaged. Our lives, as well as our bank accounts, were completely separate and I was handling my own finances as well as my own expenses. The one and only remaining tie to each other were the children.

I took a quick look at the clock. It was already 11:10 and I needed to shower before taking the kids horseback riding at 11:30. I put my phone on the charger and headed for the second floor bathroom. From the shower stall I thought I heard the distinctive ring that alerted me to incoming calls from Ross, but he and his girlfriend, Laura, were in Las Vegas so it was strange for him to be calling unless something was wrong. I grabbed a towel and ran downstairs before it could go to voicemail.

"Ross?"

"Mom!" He was shouting and sounded out of breath. "Have you talked to dad?"

"Why would I talk to your dad?" Richard and I had minimal contact now that attorneys were involved and we were seeing our own individual therapists. In fact the last time I saw him was when my furniture was being moved into storage. He was there to make sure I would pay for the movers with my own money and he wouldn't be billed.

"Mom!!!" Ross's voice bordered on hysteria.

"Ross, why would I talk to your dad?"

"I just talked to Carrie." It took me a second to register who Carrie was. She was a friend of Ross's who lived in the house next to us when we lived on Ranch Road.

"Carrie said their were television news people at her house this morning asking questions about us. They started talking to her dad wanting to know what kind of neighbors we were."

"What? Why?" Why in the world would anyone be wanting to find out what kind of neighbors we were? We hadn't seen Carrie or her family for years.

"The police found dad's car burnt up."

"What???" Oh my God, Ross." My mind was reeling. "Do you want me to fly you home?"

"No, I'm already *on* my way home. Laura's driving." Well, thank God his girlfriend was behind the wheel. Ross sounded frantic. In my head I'm trying to do the math and figure if he could make the five-plus-hour drive back to San Diego faster than it would take him to get to the airport for the next flight out.

"Mom????" I realized he was still talking. He sounded irritated that I couldn't give him any information.

"Ross I'm at Kathy's taking care of her girls for the weekend. I'll call her and see if there's someone I can get to come take over for me. Then I'll go to police station and find out what's going on."

I put my face in my hands. *Dear Lord, now what? What's happened, and why would Carrie call Ross and tell him something like that over the phone? It's not as if they were best friends. I don't think they even kept in touch after going off to different colleges.* I quickly dressed, called Kathy, and told her all hell was breaking loose. "I'm coming home," she said without hesitation. "I'll call my father-in-law to come get the girls. Hang tight. He'll be there as soon as he can."

July 16th, noon

"9-1-1 what's your emergency?"

"Have you had any reports of a car fire?"

"No ma'am."

"Are you sure? I'm calling because… because it could be my husband."

"No, ma'am, we haven't."

Kathy's father picked up the girls so I grabbed my keys and raced to the car heading for our old neighborhood. I barely had the car in park before jumping out and running up the driveway toward Carrie's house. In my haste I left without even putting on my shoes and the black asphalt was burning the soles of my feet.

I started banging on the door and calling Carrie's name. "Is your dad here?" I asked when she opened the door.

"No."

"What did you find out from the news people this morning? And why would you call Ross without knowing what was happening, Carrie, why?"

"I don't know... I don't know, Mrs. Dowell," she kept shaking her head no and seemed near tears. I was afraid I was scaring her.

"What did you hear them tell your dad?"

"They said they found your husband's car with a dead body in it. It was burnt up."

I felt the ground move beneath my feet and reached out to hold onto the doorframe to steady myself.

"But I just called the police and they don't have a report of this," I said, turning away from her before she could respond. I backed out of the driveway and headed for the police station, pulling over into the mall parking lot when I remembered the police station recently moved and I had no idea where they moved to.

I punched in Ross's number.

"Ross I'm going to the police station," I said when he answered.

"Just *forget* it mom," Ross was screaming at me. He was furious that I wasn't able to tell him what was going on and he was 300 miles away. The kids already blamed me for the separation and pending divorce, now Ross received terrible, frightening news that I couldn't verify or deny.

I called my friend Bobbie. "Bobbie, my life has just fallen apart. I don't know if Richard is burned up in a car or what's happened."

"What?"

"I have to get to the police station but they moved and I don't know where it is. Can you get an address for me." Bobbie shouted to her husband who was on the computer and returned a few seconds later with an address. It was only ten minutes away. "I'll meet you there," Bobbie said before hanging up. Within seconds, Jill's husband called.

"Queen," he used the name my students affectionately called me. "Are you driving?" I told him I was. "You need to pull over."

"What's going on?" I asked, shouting.

"You need to pull over," he said calmly.

I pulled into a small spot that offered a tiny sliver of shade. God it was so *hot.*

"Billy I can't talk now. Ross got this phone call from his friend that lived next to us on Ranch Road. I need to get to the police station... "

"Let me *talk*," Billy shouted over me.

"No," I said, angry that he thought what he had to say was more important than what I was trying to tell him. "I'm telling you what I'm *doing* right now." There was a moment of silence and I heard Billy breathe in, then slowly exhale.

"You need to pull over Queen."

"I got a call from the medical examiner."

"What's a medical examiner?" I never even *heard* of a medical examiner so didn't know why he said it so casually.

"Well, the medical examiner is the person who ... " he hedged. "They think they found Richard burned up in his car."

I blurted out, "You know Billy, Ross tried to tell me this but the police say no... no Billy. I called them. That's why I'm on my way over to the police station to try to find out what's going on."

"Well... you know the medical examiner is *like* the police."

"Then why wouldn't they know?"

"Because it happened in San Diego, Luanna."

"In San Diego? Why would Richard be in San Diego?"

"QUEEN," he said louder, and sounding irritated, like he was talking to a child.

"Who was Richard's dentist? I told them I thought it was Dr. B."

"It's not Dr. B. Dr. B is *my* dentist. And why are they calling *you*? Why aren't they calling me?" Now I was not only confused but angry.

"I don't know, Luanna."

"Well, this is bizarre. Why are they calling you?" I asked again, more to myself than him, then realized that my old cell phone number was on everything that Richard and I ever owned together. When I went and got my own phone with a new number I never gave it to Richard, and never called him from my cellphone so he couldn't store it in his contacts list. My old cellphone number must still be in Richard's phone. If he *had* burned up in a fire how could his phone possibly survive? I asked Billy, not really expecting an answer.

"He left his phone at the condo, Queen."

Since Billy called had Jill also heard the news? Things were quickly going from bad to worse.

I sat motionless in the car. I didn't know what to do. Should I continue on my way to the police station? Go back to Coronado and wait for Ross? Go to Jill and Billy's? I turned the car around and headed back to Bobbie's. I called and told her not to meet me at the police station. I would meet her back at her house. From what Billy said it sounded like the Escondido police wouldn't be able to tell me a thing.

2:00 p.m.

I knocked on Bobbie's door and a stranger answered. *"Who are you?"* I was so frantic I thought I was at the wrong house. "Where's Bobbie and Paul?" I felt things begin to spin.

"I'm their nephew, Brian," he said. "I'm visiting my aunt and uncle with my daughter." I have no doubt that God placed Brian there for me at Bobbie and Paul's. He was studying to be a fireman and knew the signs of someone going into shock. "I need to… I need to… I think my husband just killed himself." Brian took my arm and took me inside to the sofa. He brought me a glass of water and had me put my head back while he coached me through slow and measured breathing.

"He burned himself up in his car but I can't get anyone to give me any answers." I remembered the phone in my hand. "It's new and I don't remember how to … "

"Here, give it me," he said, and I handed it to this complete stranger who I knew was going to help me. "Who do you want me to call?"

I gave him a sticky note I was holding. There was a number on it I didn't remember writing. I must have written it while talking to Billy. Brian punched in the number and handed the phone to me. The trembling in my hands seemed less severe.

"This is Mrs. Dowell," I said. "Who is this?"

The woman on the other end was curt, her voice agitated. "I have been trying to reach you, Mrs. Dowell," she said without identifying herself, "and have left you messages. Who was your husband's dentist? It was *not* Dr. B."

"No… Dr. B is *my* dentist," I told her. *Think… think…* I was willing my brain to kick into gear. Then I remembered I had a few disposable toothbrushes in a travel bag I kept in my car for long days at school. "Hang on." I handed the phone to Brian and ran out to the car. Again the heat seared my feet. I would need to see if Bobbie had shoes I could borrow. I grabbed the bag from the trunk and ran back into the house. I ripped the cellophane from the brush and handed it to Brian to read to her. I heard him give her the name and phone number.

"She wants to talk to you," he said handing the phone back to me.

"Do you want to see the crime scene?" she asked without emotion.

"No, I don't want to see anything," it came out barely a whisper.

"I have to tell you," she said after a long pause, "that your husband left one of the most inflammatory suicide letters I have ever read. It implicates you. It was truly the worst letter, *about you*, that he wrote to your children."

What??? A suicide letter? Wouldn't that have burned in the fire? As if reading my mind she said, "We've already been to his condominium. He left a number of notes on the table as well as letters addressed to your children."

I got up from the sofa and began pacing, looking at the clock. Ross would be here soon. I was a mess. I didn't realize Paul and Bobbie had returned until I realized Bobbie was pacing with me. Paul sat watching us from a chair.

"What am I going to do? What am I going to do?" I asked over and over. No one seemed able to give me an answer. Finally, Paul spoke. He said the police were involved because they thought Richard had been murdered. The medical examiner was trying to make a positive identification using Richard's dental records.

Ross finally got to Bobbie and Paul's. I'm not sure how he knew I was there. Had I called him? He grabbed my keys and said, "Get in your car. We're going to Jill's." I guess he thought he was in a better place to drive than me. When we got to Jill's she was hysterical, screaming and crying. I kept trying to calm her down telling her things were going to be okay, but she wasn't having any of it.

Still, I kept thinking this was all a mistake. Richard wouldn't do this. Since I learned he was expediting getting a new passport and had been researching Indonesia, I entertained the possibility that he might just disappear, or at the least, leave the country, but this? Never. I stood beside the chair where Jill was sobbing uncontrollably and crossed the room stopping in front of a window when a thought began to develop. *Richard was so smart... was it possible he* staged *this whole thing so he could just disappear?* All week the local news had been reporting the disappearance of a foreign exchange student went missing after hiking in the exact area where Richard's car was found. Could it be *him* in Richard's car? It sounded crazy but...

All of a sudden people began arriving. Jeri's sister, Lily, had been watching the news when Richard's driver's license photo appeared on a split screen with a burned out car. She started making phone calls and learned I was at Jill's. She and Jeri arrived just as the kids started pummeling me with questions.

"When was the last time you talked to dad?" Jill wanted to know.

"I don't remember."

"Why couldn't you have just *talked* to him? *Why?*" she asked over and over. It was heart wrenching.

"Jill you *know* why," was all I could say. I couldn't seem to process what was happening; the kids couldn't understand why I wasn't more distraught. I just kept thinking that I was all cried out. *I started crying February 23rd and didn't stop until my sadness was replaced by anger.*

Dear Jill and Ross,

Just another lonely day and a truly sad day indeed.

I was up most of the night thinking about your condo Jill and your Fidelity account Ross. I have decided that if I can end all the legal crap with our Mother, she might have the heart to give you back hour (sic) home Jill and to give you what is rightfully yours (and not hers) Ross. Your Mother has become an extremely GREEDY and UNFORGIVING person and I am not sure this final action of mine will work, but I must give it a try.

By ending the legal battle of our divorce and the injunctions against OUR money inner account and the house escrow, it will stop the bleeding of the attorney's fee, allow Mother to purchase the house and to take over my pension (over $80,000 annually) and my Social Security pension ($3460.80 annually) — this should make her a very happy woman with a very hollow victory.

As you know, we have been in and out of counseling throughout our marriage. Your Mother brought a great deal of personal baggage into our sessions that started with her first marriage. She was never able to release or let go of her baggage. Therefore, our counseling continued — she lived her life in denial that she shared in none of the responsibility for her failed marriage. She actually kept her wedding picture of them in a trunk in our garage for several years during our marriage until I saw it and questioned her about it. I share this story with you because your Mother did exactly the same thing to us. She is in total denial of any responsibility for the breakup of our marriage. I asked for very little in our marriage and received virtually nothing. We live in a DEAD SEXLESS marriage. Shortly after Ross was born she announced to me that, "Now that I have what I wanted (two kids) I don't need you anymore" and this is just how she treated me from that day forward. I did not leave the marriage because of you two and I always lived in hope that our marriage would get better —sometimes it got a little better but pretty much always the same DEAD SEXLESS marriage. She would go for endless months and even years without allowing me to make love to her. Throughout our counseling sessions this was alway an issue and she would always deny this truth. The quote about this has haunted me ever since she said it, and I do believe it carried a lot of meaning on her part and her baggage continued throughout our marriage. After well over a year of your Mother not allowing me to touch her, I stepped out of our marriage to seek non-sexual intimacy elsewhere — regardless of what she says. Again, I asked for very little and received nothing. This is where your Mother accepts no responsibility — she is really ignorant in the area of "his sexuality" as outlined in scripture. She will tell her version of our lives — you will believe your hearts. On February 23, 2010 (the day she found out) she accused me of making wrong choices. I certainly did make wrong choices. I admitted them and confessed to Christ — he died for our sins and forgave me for my sins — something your Mother refused to do — I have harbored no guilt for my transgressions. Your Mother too, made several bad choices throughout our marriage... they nude pictures with the photographer lusting over her ... the massage sessions with the masseur fondling her body parts, etc., etc., etc.

I am sorry I have to be so graphic, but you needed to hear my side of the story to really know that your Mother was not the perfect woman that she will try to convince you she is and that she shares equally in the destruction of our marriage and family — it all could have been saved with the simple words, I forgive you." ... I forgave her!

I was thinking seriously of taking both our lives but I could not take both your parents from you.

Please ask your Mother to use the death benefits from my STRS pension and my Social Security to finish the CREAMATION process and just scatter my ashes anywhere legal. If you Mother is too greedy to do this, I will leave it up to you two to think of something. Please do not have a service of any kind — I have made my peace with GOD.

Ross you lost a friend... last year, therefore, you know that all it takes is time for emotions to wane and heal. In just a few short weeks your Dad will be just a memory. So please, Jill and Ross be strong and always be there for each other. Jill hold tightly to Billy for he is a good man — the best! Ross, what you need to strive for is that advanced degree — make sure you achieve that goal — for your Dad and especially for yourself… our memorie are all we ever have left in our lives — please keep me in yours.

Ross and Jill, try to forgive your Mother and when this has all passed try to love her unconditionally… for it will be just a few short years before her passing… it is sad that she developed such a DARK and GREEDY HEART…but then it was her choice.

I will truly miss the two of you — I love you both so very much. Life is so empty for me now and I no longer have the will to live.

With much Love and Emotion,

Dad

Chapter Twenty One

July 17, 2010

I don't remember how, but I ended up at Jeri's sleeping on the floor. Ross spent the night at Jill and Billy's. Jill had insisted we clean out Richard's condo in the morning. I couldn't understand the urgency and thought we should wait but I could see Jill was barely holding it together and thought if being in "charge" of something would help her cope, then I would acquiesce. She'd been stuttering when she repeated, "I want to clean it out. I want to clean it out," insisting over and over that we get his clothes ready to donate. She never stuttered before and it was scaring me.

Saturday morning Jill called to make sure I was awake and to tell me that Ross and Billy had been up drinking all night and would meet us at the condo later. I hoped that meant we'd put off the task until either later in the day or do it an entirely different day, but Jill was on a mission and wouldn't be deterred. We arrived at Richard's condo but when I opened the door to get out Jill said I wasn't allowed to go up. I was ready to argue about her going in alone just as Ross's truck pulled in beside us. Ross knew where Richard hid a spare key and went to retrieve it from the garage. This was not going to go well.

I sat in Jill's car waiting. I knew that going into their father's condo would be difficult, but knowing that Richard chose to end his own life made it all the more painful. What had he left behind for them to find? I found out that the medical examiner already read the suicide letter to Jill over the phone, which I found not only unprofessional, but unforgivable. Apparently Jill told her that Richard and I were "in the middle" of a divorce, so

I can only assume she saw that as a green light to disclose the suicide note. *It's only been 14 days since I signed the divorce papers,* I thought, *and she saw that as the middle?*

All of a sudden Jill appeared beside the car.

"You can come up."

I took a deep breath before crossing the threshold to where Richard spent the last days of his life, praying silently for God to give me the strength to do this. Ross was on the couch. His eyes were expressionless as he stared off into space. Jill dropped to her knees, sobbing, then start hitting the floor saying, "Daddy why would you do this to us?" I could smell cigarettes which surprised me because Richard didn't smoke.

Ross stood and looked at me. "I can't do this," he said, turned, and walked out the door. *We shouldn't be doing this now,* I keep thinking, then had an unsettling thought. Paul said the police were involved because they thought this may have been a murder. If we cleaned out the condo would that be tampering with evidence? Could I go to prison? I was willing to take the risk it would keep Jill from going over the edge. Still... I turned and looked at the door. Wouldn't the police have put yellow crime scene tape across the door if they were still investigating?

I turned back toward Jill who was standing at the kitchen table. Richard had divided it into two sections; one half for Jill, the other half for Ross. There were at least 50 yellow "sticky notes" covering the surface. Richard's wallet was on Ross's side with a hand-written note saying he was sorry that was all the money he had to leave him. His cell phone was also on the table.

On Jill's side Richard left the books he bought for me that I refused to read: Dr. Laura Schlessinger's, "*How to Keep Your Husband Happy*" and others. Richard already gave Jill one of the books I rejected, highlighted things he thought she needed to know. *Please don't tell me you're leaving these sick "instructions" for your own daughter,* I thought. But there they were, in highlighted detail, of what he thought a wife should do for her husband… a more in-depth explanation of the "wifely duties" I refused to perform. Dr. Laura's book was open. At least 50 pages had sticky notes attached.

I pulled one of the notes from Ross's side of the table. "First you have to call AAA abut the car insurance," it read. *Are you kidding me?* He wanted Ross to put in a claim for his burned up car? "Cancel SDGE," instructed another; "Here's the guy's name I rented the place from. He should give you my deposit back. Here's his number," and on and on. He put Jill in charge of whatever service would be conducted and what was to be done with his remains. "I want no decisions made by your mother. She can pay for it. She can afford it."

Jill seemed almost in a trance.

"Jill," I said, somewhat harshly, trying to snap her out of the place she was wallowing in. "Where do we start?" I needed to bring her back to the task at hand, the task *she* insisted we start *immediately*.

"The closet."

We walked into the bedroom, paused, then opened the closet door. Jill is *immediately* overwhelmed and, I have to admit, *so am I*. I touch the neatly hung shirts and pants that I knew so well, clothes I bought him during better times. I felt my breathing become shallow and focused on deep, slow breaths. *Oh my God,* I thought. *I know what he was wearing to his suicide.* I knew because these were missing from his wardrobe. Each had some special memory.

"Jill..." I said turning toward her. "We can't do this, you and me, alone. We need some back up. I need to call in my troops." She didn't respond at first but I needed to stand my ground. This was bigger than the two of us. *"Please."*

"Yes," she finally whispered. I called Jackie, Jeff and Linda.

By the time Jackie and Jeff arrived Jill had returned to her cocoon of anguish and grief. Jeff led her down the outside stairs of the complex and comforted her the best he could. Jill knew Jeff her entire life so it was easy for her to see him as a paternal figure. Jill's grief, however, quickly turned to anger, and that anger was directed toward me. She wouldn't let me touch anything in Richard's condo.

After packing the closet, Jill sat down at Richard's desk. I stood behind her, somewhat uncomfortable that my *child* was going through our personal papers that included financial documents and personal correspondences…

"Jill," I said when she gave a cursory glance to a folder and tossed it aside.

"Those cancelled checks and stubs are mine. I would like to have them," I said.

"Dad doesn't want you to have *anything*," she said, defiantly. *Still…*

"Then you can stand here while I take the things I need to have," and she did.

I left with my check stubs, any documents I would need for taxes, and legal documents that had my signature.

With the help of Jackie, Jeff and Linda, we cleaned out the condo to Jill's satisfaction, but when she wanted to put all of Richard's things in a storage facility I put my foot down. "I have free storage and could store his things with mine," but she refused. "Then you'll have to pay to store his things."

"Fine," she said with obvious disgust. "*I'll* pay for it."

October, 2010

"You need to know there has been *no stone* unturned in your life," a detective from the San Diego Police Department told me. I was contacted and asked to come to the police station for the "official report" of Richard's death.

I blinked several times and looked from the folder in my hand to the detective's face. It never dawned on me that they might have thought I had something to do with Richard's death, perhaps because of my severe allergic reaction to gasoline, which they determined Richard used to douse his body and car outside and then inside before striking the match. My reaction to gasoline is so severe I actually have a handicap placard for an attendant to pump gas for me. Even fumes send me into anaphylactic shock. *So gasoline? Really?* Certainly there were easier ways to end one's life. Was his choice his final *fuck you, Luanna?* Or was it Richard's way of absolving me of any part of his decision to end his life?

I guess I will never know.

Epilogue July, 2014

It has been four years since Richard decided to end his life. I will never know whether that decision was easier than living with his sexual addiction or the reality that his addiction had been exposed.

While my children still need to place blame, there has been much healing during the past four years. We scattered Richard's ashes in his homeland of South Dakota, a painful journey and return to where his life began. Richard had come full circle. Slowly and steadily I continue rebuilding my relationship with our children. There are still many things they don't know about their father but unless there is information that could positively impact their lives I have no need to share any more of the negative than they already know. Richard will always be their father and they will always hold a special place for him in their hearts.

I've been asked why I would want my story to become public and the answer is, and isn't, simple. First and foremost I would have never survived if it wasn't for my faith. I truly believe that God led me to discover, in His perfect timing, the secret life Richard was leading, and then provided me with friends and *total strangers* who taught and helped me survive. If even one person sees themselves within these pages and is able to free themselves from a destructive relationship or realizes that they need to be less submissive whether physically, emotionally or financially, than I consider sharing my story as *paying it forward*.

Resources

When a person decides to take their own life they have "completed" suicide, not committed suicide. The terminology is such because they took their own life and no one else's, so did not "commit" a crime.

If you are the survivor of a loved one who completed suicide, you have become part of a club you never asked to join. There is no correct way to grieve, so there may be many people who can't understand your emotions, or lack of emotion. There are many organizations available to help survivors, whether the death was of a spouse, a parent, a sibling, a child or even a friend. There are also many organizations available to help those who find themselves victims of sexual addictions. Know you are not alone.

Survivors of Suicide Loss (SOSL)
info@soslsd.org

Out of the Darkness (coping with suicide loss)
www.outofthedarkness.org
(855) 869-2377

National Suicide Prevention Lifeline
www.suicidepreventionlifeline.org
1-800-273-TALK (8255)

American Foundation for Suicide Prevention
info@afsp.org
(888) 333-2377

Sex and Love Addicts Anonymous (SLAA)
www.slaafws.org

Sexual Recovery Institute
www.sexualrecovery.com
(877) 958-8032

recovery.org (Inpatient treatment centers for addictions)
www.recovery.org
1-888-298-6689

Made in the USA
San Bernardino, CA
22 January 2015